THE VOCATION LECTURES

MAX WEBER

THE VOCATION LECTURES

"Science as a Vocation"
"Politics as a Vocation"

Edited and with an Introduction by
David Owen and Tracy B. Strong

Translation by
Rodney Livingstone

Hackett Publishing Company
Indianapolis/Cambridge

08 07 06 05 04   1 2 3 4 5 6 7 8

For further information, please address
Hackett Publishing Company, Inc.
P. O. Box 44937
Indianapolis, Indiana 46244–0937

www.hackettpublishing.com

Cover design by Listenberger Design Associates
Interior design by Abigail Coyle
Composition by William Hartman
Printed at Maple-Vail Book Manufacturing

Library of Congress Cataloging-in-Publication Data

Weber, Max 1864–1920.
    [Wissenschaft als Beruf. English]
    The vocation lectures / Max Weber ; edited and with an
introduction by David Owen and Tracy B. Strong ; translation
by Rodney Livingstone.
        p. cm.
    Includes bibliographical references and index.
    Contents: Science as a vocation — Politics as a vocation.
    ISBN 0-87220-666-1 (cloth) — ISBN 0-87220-665-3 (pbk.)
    1. Science as a profession.   2. Politics, Practical.
I. Owen, David.   II. Strong, Tracy B.   III. Livingstone, Rodney.
IV. Weber, Max, 1864–1920. Politik als Beruf. English.   V. Title.

Q147.W413 2004
502'.3—dc22
                                                      2003057070

∞

In memory of Irving Velody

CONTENTS

Introduction   ix
A Note on the Translation   lxiii
Texts of Weber in German   lxiv
Major Texts of Weber in English   lxvi
Further Reading   lxviii

Science as a Vocation   1

Politics as a Vocation   32

Name Index   95
Subject Index   98

INTRODUCTION

Max Weber's Calling to Knowledge and Action

> It might be a basic characteristic of existence that
> those who would know it completely would perish,
> in which case the strength of a spirit should be
> measured according to how much of the "truth"
> one could still barely endure.
>
> F. Nietzsche, *Beyond Good and Evil*,
> paragraph 39

Max Weber has claim not only to being one of the founders of modern social science but also to being one of the most acute diagnosticians of the conditions of modernity in the West. The fifty-six years of his life saw the writing of an astonishing array of works, not only in the general field of political economy (ranging from ancient Rome through the Middle Ages to contemporary Europe and America), but also in philosophy, the methodology of social scientific investigation, musicology, the sociology of most of the world's major religions, social theory, and political science. Nor were his efforts purely "academic": as what we would now call a "public intellectual," his attentions included contemporary events. For instance, after the 1905 abortive revolution in Russia, he took six months to learn Russian so that he could read the sources in the original language and then produced several important analyses of those events. A man of impeccably bourgeois origins and upbringing, he was also at the intersection of several of the most progressive dimensions of German and European intellectual, cultural, and artistic life.

Weber is also one of the few scholars of a century ago with whom most contemporary social scientists still feel the need to come to terms. In preparing the (necessarily dramatically incomplete) Further Reading section of this volume, we were struck by how many modern scholars, as well as those of previous and later generations, have written on Weber, even, and perhaps notably, when he did not remain the primary focus of the work for which they are best known.[1] Weber was and remains a giant—an unavoidable figure for serious scholars.

* * *

Max Weber was born Karl Emil Maximilian Weber on April 21, 1864, the oldest of the eight children of Max and Helene Weber. His university studies at Heidelberg were interrupted in 1883 for a year of military service. He passed examinations for the civil service in 1886 and by 1891 took his *Habilitation* with a work on Roman agrarian history, thus qualifying himself as a university lecturer. In 1893 he was appointed to a chair as professor of law and economics at the University of Berlin, and he married his second cousin, Marianne Schnitger, the daughter of the country doctor Eduard Schnitger and Eleonore Weber. The next year he was called to a chair at the University of Freiburg in political science (*Staatswissenschaft*): his inaugural lecture was an analysis of the German situation entitled "The National State and Economic Policy."[2] The year 1897 saw the death of his father, from whom he had been estranged for some time. Shortly thereafter he moved to a new chair at the University of Heidelberg, but during the following year he sank into a clinical depression and took leave of his university duties. He did not begin to emerge from the depression until 1902.[3] On the occasion of a scientific congress at the 1904 World's Fair in St. Louis, he visited the United States. Accepting a position as "honorary professor" at Heidelberg, he did not return to university duties, but writings nonetheless poured from his pen. Scholarly books and articles appeared continuously, including what became his most famous work, *The Protestant Ethic and the Spirit of Capitalism,* as did newspaper articles, reviews, and polemical exchanges.

His aims were not just "academic," although they were always pursued with a high degree of intellectual rigor. An important part of his work, as he conceived of it, was to promote the political

---

[1] For a full demonstration of this point, see Alan Sica, *Max Weber: A Comprehensive Bibliography* (Transaction Publishers, forthcoming 2003).

[2] "Der Nationalstaat und die Volkswirtschaftspolitik," in Max Weber, *Gesammelte Politische Schriften* (Tübingen: Mohr, 1958), pp. 7–30 (henceforth GPS), translated in Peter Lassman and Ronald Speirs, eds., *Weber: Political Writings* (Cambridge: Cambridge University Press, 1994), pp. 1–28 (henceforth PW).

[3] For a provocative account of Weber's mental illness, see Arthur Mitzman, *The Iron Cage: An Historical Interpretation of Max Weber* (New York: Grossett and Dunlap, 1971).

education of the German public, an education he felt sadly lacking in the aftermath of the long rule of Otto von Bismarck. Bismarck, in Weber's later analysis, had by his very political genius given rise to a situation in which no one could possibly take his place and for which his policies had ensured that none would have adequate training in responsibility and political experience to assume leadership.[4] After examining what hopes there might be for political leadership from each of the German classes, he concluded his inaugural lecture with the assertion that none of them would be up to the dangers confronting Germany and that the country thus faced "a monstrous work of *political* education."[5] This concern remained with him throughout his life: by the end of World War I he had established himself as Germany's single most respected voice on public affairs.

To this end, in addition to his writings, he was actively involved with several political groups that ranged over the entire political spectrum. He never ran for nor held office himself, despite the fact that, as his wife wrote in his biography, he had "always admired the captain of a ship, who held the destiny of so many in his hand."[6] During World War I he not only saw (limited) service as a hospital orderly but also published a series of articles analyzing Germany's conduct, policies, and war aims. He accompanied the German delegation to Versailles for the peace talks and tried thereafter to persuade General Ludendorff to take public responsibility for the defeat. On June 14, 1920, he died of a lung infection consequent to influenza. He was the most influential intellectual in Germany at the time.

Like some of the other great thinkers of his time (Nietzsche, Marx, and Freud come most readily to mind), some aspects of his thought have passed into common parlance. When we speak of charismatic leaders or bewail bureaucracy, we do so in language that has its origin in Weber's work. When contemporary politicians or cultural critics call for a return to the "Protestant ethic" (or nondenominationally, the "work ethic"), they echo Weber's analysis, though as we shall see, generally without his sense of the tragic. He is one of the handful of thinkers whose thought has permanently shaped the way in which we think of our modern world.

---

[4] See the magisterial article "Parlament und Regierung im neugeordneten Deutschland" (1918) in GPS 126–336, translated in PW and in Max Weber, *Economy and Society*, vol. 2 (Berkeley and Los Angeles: University of California Press, 1978). See also Henry Kissinger, "Bismarck: The White Revolutionary," *Daedalus* 97, no. 3 (Summer 1961): 888–924, which takes over Weber's argument.

[5] "The National State and the National Economy," GPS 29.

[6] Marianne Weber, *Max Weber: A Biography* (New York: Wiley, 1975).

The "Vocation" Lectures

The lectures in this volume are work at (although not of) the end of Weber's life. They reflect and encapsulate the commanding central project of his entire career, as he understood himself to have pursued it. This project was to understand how it is that "in the West alone there have appeared cultural manifestations that—at least we like to tell ourselves this—in their development go in the direction of universal significance and validity."[7] Weber's explicit concerns in these works are with the nature and status of science—most especially its desire to claim final authority for itself—and of political claims and political action—most especially the desire to rest political matters on moral certainties or justification.[8] As he sought to discover how this development had occurred, however, so also did he endeavor to explicate what he understood as its importance to human life in the West.[9] This enterprise of a life's work is distilled into these lectures. They constitute not only the most succinct account of his knowledge, but they also express more clearly than anywhere else in his published material his understanding of his own vocation, his own life. As such they form a whole and constitute not so much a summary of his work as an exploration of its implications for human existence.[10]

Both of these lectures are about "vocation" or *Beruf*. The term has the everyday meaning of "profession" but carries with it also the resonances from its religious origin as "calling." Weber intends both meanings. In *The Protestant Ethic and the Spirit of Capitalism*[11] he recognizes the religious origins and tone of the word—a "task given

---

[7] Max Weber, *Religionssoziologie* (Mohr: Tübingen, 1988), vol. 1, p. 1: "gerade auf dem Boden des Okzidents, und nur hier, Kulturerscheinungen auftraten, welche doch—wie wenigstens wir uns gern vorstellen—in einer Entwicklungsrichtung von universeller Bedeutung und Gültigkeit lagen." This passage is problematically translated and misleadingly placed as the introduction to Talcott Parsons' edition and translation of *The Protestant Ethic and the Spirit of Capitalism* (New York: Scribner's, 1958), p. 13 (henceforth PESC).

[8] For example, in "The Future Form of the German State," Weber accuses Woodrow Wilson of having brought not peace but "unending struggle" (GPS 349); see also "On the Matter of War Guilt," GPS 381 ff.

[9] On these matters see Harvey Goldman, *Politics, Death, and the Devil: Self and Power in Max Weber and Thomas Mann* (Berkeley and Los Angeles: University of California Press, 1992).

[10] Joachim Vahland (*Max Webers entzauberte Welt* [Würzburg: Königsheim and Neumann, 2001]) insightfully uses the idea of Weber as a *Berufsmensch* to analyze his thought.

[11] *Religionssoziologie*, vol. 1, p. 63 (PESC 79 ff).

by God," as he terms it. Weber asserts that the concept of calling is particular to Protestantism and in a lengthy footnote goes to some pains to differentiate it from more cosmically and less individually ordered concepts in the Roman Catholicism of someone like St. Thomas Aquinas.[12] Just as importantly, however, Weber differentiates the Puritan or Calvinist notion of *Beruf* from the Lutheran conception of a calling as a "stroke of fate" (*Schickung*)—something that happens to one and into which one must fit and be content. In Calvinism, however, vocation is a "command of God to an individual to work to His glory."[13] In the "Science" lecture Weber tellingly used the word "*hingeben*" in relation to the youth who "gives over" his life to *Wissenschaft*. *Hingeben* carries connotations of sacrifice and is the term that a woman might use (or be thought to use) in speaking of "giving herself to a man." Vocation is thus both active and passive—one must freely give oneself to that which calls one, which by the acknowledgment of that call appears as and becomes one's own. As a free act, vocation is thus defining of the person; as a necessary act, it is expressive of the person. Vocational activity has as itself nothing of the instrumental; it is an end in itself (thus in some sense moral) but without reference to any grounding or act other than the freely chosen commitment of individuals to their own particular fates.

Both lectures were occasioned by invitations from Immanuel Birnbaum, rector of the University of Munich, to participate in a public forum series on "*geistige Arbeit als Beruf*"—"intellectual or spiritual work as a calling"—which had been organized by the Freistudentische Bund, a left-liberal student association. Whereas Weber seems to have been reluctant to give the second of his two lectures (see the discussion of the "Politics" lecture below), we have no reason to suspect any similar reluctance concerning the delivery of the "Science" lecture; indeed, it is hard to see how the organizers of the series could have come up with a topic more likely to engage Weber's intellectual passion. The immediate intellectual context of the lecture is provided, as Wolfgang Schluchter has noted, by Alexander Schwab's essay "Vocation and Youth," in which Schwab, a student of Weber's economist brother Alfred, had presented commitment to a calling as incompatible with conduct according to the proper ethos of science.[14] Weber was to take a different tack.

---

[12] Ibid., p. 70n5 (PESC 80).

[13] Ibid., p. 172 (PESC 170).

[14] See Wolfgang Schluchter, "The Question of the Dating of 'Science as a Vocation' and 'Politics as a Vocation,'" in Schluchter, 1981: 113–6.

In part as consequence of the fact that these lectures were originally published as separate pamphlets and then in two separate German volumes of Weber's works, one dedicated to his "political"
writings and the other to his "scientific" work, and in part as consequence of a positivistic conceptual separation of "facts" from "values," the close relation of these lectures to each other has often been
obscured. Wolfgang Schluchter is quite correct when, in his after-
word to the *Studienausgabe* edition of the lectures, he notes that
they are both "key texts to [Weber's] answers to the central questions of modern culture." These texts, he continues, are in fact neither to be assimilated with Weber's more explicitly methodological
writings on the one hand, nor, on the other, to his more topical political articles. "They pursue another goal," he writes; "they are 'philosophical' texts, with which they lead at once to the acknowledgment
of that which is [*Tatsachenerkenntnis*] and of the self and at the
same time persuade the individual to responsible work in the service
of a suprapersonal cause [*Sache*]."[15]

If these are "philosophical" texts, however, what kind of philosophy are they? One should think of them as a form of "radical Kantianism,"[16] and in this sense they are the inheritor and continuation
of a line of philosophical inquiry that starts in the seventeenth century, achieves its classic formulation in Kant, and then provides a
continuing counterpoint to the Hegelianism of the nineteenth century.[17] Kant sought in his *Critiques* to explore the conditions of how
a given human activity was possible. Thus the first *Critique* (of Pure
Reason) answers the question of "how is knowledge of nature possible" and proceeds not by giving one knowledge of nature but by
making critically clear what has to be the case for such knowledge to

---

[15] Wolfgang Schluchter, "Nachwort," to Max Weber, *Wissenschaft als Beruf (1917/
1919) Politik als Beruf (1919)*, ed. Wolfgang J. Mommsen and Wolfgang Schluchter
with the collaboration of Birgitt Morgenbrod (Tübingen: Mohr, 1994), p. 91.
Schluchter is influenced by the dissertation of Dieter Henrich, *Die Einheit der Wissenschaftslehre Max Webers* (Tübingen, 1952), who in turn was influenced by Karl
Löwith.

[16] Raymond Aron, in his introduction to a French edition of these lectures (*Le
Savant et le Politique* [Paris: Plon, 1959], p. 55), calls Weber a Kantian. Vahland
(see note 10) analyzes Weber as belonging to the Kantian and neo-Kantian tradition
(esp. chapters 5 and 7).

[17] Weber in fact rarely mentions Hegel, and when he does he speaks with distress
about the influence of Hegel on German and European thought. See Paul Honigsheim,
On Max Weber (New York: Free Press, 1968), p. 12; see W. Schluchter, *The Rise of
Western Rationalism: Max Weber's Developmental History,* trans. G. Roth (Berkeley and Los Angeles: University of California Press, 1981), p. 21.

in fact occur. Kant refers to such awareness of the conditions of knowledge as "transcendental." In this spirit, one might read Weber's lectures as having inherited this critical and transcendental[18] tradition and thus as respective answers to the questions "What can I possibly know?" and "What can I possibly do?"

What, however, makes Weber's work *radical* Kantianism"? For something to be "radical" Kantianism, it must nonetheless participate in Kant's basic approach to philosophical activity, that is, the critique. One might identify several kinds of critique, each progressively more "radical."[19] The first level—apparent, one might say, in Montaigne, or in a different way in Hume—consists in the realization that humans make unpredictable and repeated errors in their understanding of the world, errors that the experience of the world does not automatically correct. Typically such errors consist in attributing categorical status to some activity of human understanding—thinking that such and such activity is, for instance, ultimately morally justified. Hume and Montaigne—to whose names one could add those of Pascal and Montesquieu, among many others—sought to establish the nature and kind of the most usual errors made in asserting judgments about the world, be they epistemological or practical. The position entailed by this level of critique is skepticism. Hume found that he could escape the skeptical mode and conclusions only by removing himself from philosophical reflection. Reason was itself no anchor because, as he wrote, it was not "contrary to reason for him to prefer the destruction of the whole world to prevent the merest scratching of his little finger."[20] As he wrote in the *Treatise of Human Nature*:

> Most fortunately it happens, that since reason is incapable of dispelling these clouds, Nature herself suffices to that purpose, and cures me of this philosophical melancholy and delirium, either by relaxing this bent of mind, or by some avocation, and lively impression of my senses, which obliterate all these chimeras. I dine, I play a game of backgammon, I converse, and am merry with my friends; and when, after three or four hours' amusement, I would return to

---

[18] Technically Weber's is not "transcendental" since it remains beholden in his science to the "empirical world." We might call it "quasi-transcendental" or "heuristically transcendental."

[19] We are influenced here by Dieter Henrich, *Aesthetic Judgment and the Moral Image of the World* (Stanford, CA: Stanford University Press, 1992), pp. 71 ff.

[20] David Hume, *Treatise of Human Nature* (New York: Penguin, 1985), book 2, part 3, section 3, p. 463.

these speculations, they appear so cold, and strained, and ridiculous, that I cannot find in my heart to enter into them any further.[21]

Here the critique serves to establish an unbridgeable distance between philosophical thought and the conduct of life. For Humean skepticism, philosophy cannot be the realm from which one might expect a provision of adequate answers as to what to do. Weber shares this sense of the limitation of knowledge for the deepest questions of human existence.

A second level of critique comes in the realization that it is not just that the mind itself may make errors in its understanding of the world but that the source of these errors itself may be built into the paths that reason must follow by virtue of what it is. Thus famously in the *Critique of Pure Reason* (1781) Kant established that reason was itself limited and that this limitation was not a fault of reason but rather made it possible for rationality to exist at all. Two years later, in section 32 of the *Prolegomena to Any Future Metaphysics*, he gave his earlier argument a succinct formulation:

Since the oldest days of philosophy inquirers into pure reason have conceived, besides the things of sense, or appearances (phenomena), which make up the sensible world, certain creations of the understanding [*Verstandeswesen*], called noumena, which should constitute an intelligible world. And as appearance and illusion were by those men identified (a thing which we may well excuse in an undeveloped epoch), actuality was only conceded to the creations of thought.

And we indeed, rightly considering objects of sense as mere appearances, confess thereby that they are based upon a thing in itself, though we know not this thing in its internal constitution, but only know its appearances, viz., the way in which our senses are affected by this unknown something. The understanding therefore, by assuming appearances, grants the existence of things in themselves also, and so far we may say, that the representation of such things as form the basis of phenomena, consequently of mere creations of the understanding, is not only admissible, but unavoidable.

Our critical deduction by no means excludes things of that sort (noumena), but rather limits the principles of the Aesthetic (the science of the sensibility) to this, that they shall not extend to all things, as everything would then be turned into mere appearance, but that they shall only hold good of objects of possible experience. Hereby then objects of the understanding are granted, but with the inculcation of this rule which admits of no exception:

[21] Ibid., book 1, part 4, section 7, p. 316.

"that we neither know nor can know anything at all definite of these pure objects of the understanding, because our pure concepts of the understanding as well as our pure intuitions extend to nothing but objects of possible experience, consequently to mere things of sense, and as soon as we leave this sphere these concepts retain no meaning whatever."[22]

Kant claims here what he had established earlier in the *Critique:* that all experience is experience of and only of appearances; that whatever it is that appearances are of is something that cannot be the object of experience; that we can only know how it is that we have experiences; and that it is in reflecting on how it is that we have experience of appearances that we can ground reason. This, then, is a second level of critique, in which secure knowledge is seen to be found only in the critical reflection upon insecure experience. It held that there was a realm of knowledge that, while necessary for human beings, was not accessible to human experience. In his theory of ideal types, Weber will attempt the construction of the equivalent of a noumenal realm for the purposes of making social science possible.[23] It is for this reason that we call his understanding "heuristically transcendental" (see note 18).

Kant's accomplishment was instantly recognized as the source of a radically new conception of philosophy—one that while admitting the full force of skepticism would nonetheless not remain mired in it. The *third* level of critique is its radicalization into the suspicion and argument that the structures of reason itself are also the *sources* of deceptions, deceptions made all the more powerful by the fact that we are unable to resist them. Nietzsche, who can stand in here for a stable of other nineteenth-century thinkers such as Novalis, Schiller, and Schopenhauer, summed up these developments in *Twilight of the Idols.* In sections three and four of "How the True World Finally Became a Fable" he writes:

3. The true world, unattainable, unprovable, unpromisable, but a consolation, an obligation, an imperative, merely by virtue of being thought. (The old sun basically, but glimpsed through fog and skepticism; the idea become sublime, pallid, Nordic, Königsbergian.)

---

[22] Immanual Kant, "Prolegomena to Any Future Metaphysics," in Carl Friedrich, ed., *Philosophy of Kant,* (New York: Modern Library, 1949), pp. 86–7.

[23] See the discussion of ideal types in Tracy B. Strong, "Max Weber and the Bourgeoisie," in Asher Horowitz and Terry Maley, eds., *The Barbarism of Reason* (Toronto: University of Toronto Press, 1994).

4. The true world—unattainable? In any case, unattained. And if it is unattained, it is also *unknown*. And hence it is not consoling, redeeming, or obligating either; to what could something unknown obligate us? . . . (Gray dawn. First yawnings of reason. Rooster's crow of positivism.)[24]

As noted, the first two kinds of critique are present in Weber's work, but it is important that he also participates at the third level. It is a dangerous level in that it is very easy to move from it to a kind of epistemological nihilism: rationality is to no avail, all is illusion and nothing has any meaning in itself.[25] This is what Nietzsche meant by the "Death of God": the human condition in which no action or claim could be understood as having reference to anything that transcended its mere existence. Weber reflects a sense of this danger from his earliest work on. In 1893, two years before his assumption of his first university appointment, while speaking on "The Agrarian Labor Question" he concludes his remarks by saying:

> You will perhaps not have completely escaped the impression that I have spoken under the weight of a certain resignation and that the challenges . . . I have sought to pose here are likewise the products of this resignation—and this is indeed the case. . . . We cannot bring back to life the naïve enthusiastic energy that animated the previous generation, for we are faced with tasks other than those our fathers had to solve. They built us a mighty house, and we are invited to take place there and be well therein. The tasks that confront us are of another kind.[26]

As he set it for himself, Weber's task was to face this increasingly widespread *Kulturpessimissus*—this incipient nihilism—head on, as

---

[24] Friedrich Nietzsche, *Twilight of the Idols*. Translated by Richard Polt and with an Introduction by Tracy B. Strong (Indianapolis: Hackett Publishing Company, 1997), p. 23.

[25] It is the sense of this that leads Leo Strauss (mistakenly) to call Weber a "nihilist" in *Natural Right and History* (Chicago: University of Chicago Press, 1953).

[26] *Gesammelte Aufsätze zur Soziologie und Sozialpolitik* (Tübingen: Mohr, 1924), pp. 467–8: "Sie werden vielleicht den Eindruck nicht ganz verloren haben, daß ich unter dem Druck einer gewissen Resignation gesprochen habe, und daß diejenigen Forderungen . . . welche ich versucht habe, hier aufzustellen, gleichfalls das Produkt einer solchen Resignation sind,—und das ist in der Tat der Fall. . . . Wir können die naive enthusiastische Tatkraft nicht wieder aufleben lassen, welche die Generation vor uns beseelte, weil wir vor Aufgaben anderer Art gestellt sind, als unsere Väter es seinerzeit gewesen sind. Sie haben um uns ein festes Haus gebaut, und wir sind eingeladen, darin Platz zu nehmen und es uns darin wohl sein zu lassen. Die Aufgaben, die uns gestellt, sind anderer Art."

he experienced it in politics, culture, science, and philosophy. The loss of the availability of meaning was for Weber an historical fact and would not disappear if one simply turned one's head away and wished for something else.

ON "SCIENCE AS A VOCATION"

The lecture "Science as a Vocation" was delivered on November 7, 1917, some fourteen months before the presentation of "Politics as a Vocation," in a war-weary—but as yet undefeated—Germany and against the immediate political backdrop of both the February and October Russian revolutions and the entry of the United States into the war the preceding April.[27] In this highly charged political context, Max Weber offers a relentlessly frank diagnosis of the external and internal conditions comprising the fate of the scholar in the contemporary world—a topic whose ethical import was immediately apparent to his contemporaries.[28] To understand the character of this act of *parrhesia,* it is worth recalling Weber's remark to a student that a modern scholar must, if he is honest, admit that "he could not have accomplished crucial parts of his own work without the contributions of Marx and Nietzsche."[29] It is so because Marx and Nietzsche pose, respectively, two questions that provide pivotal orientation points for Weber's reflections on the fate of the modern scholar: "What is the relationship between science and politics?" and "What is the meaning and value of science?" Both of the topics raised by these questions are pressing for Weber. The first compels reflection on the issue of whether science can serve as a foundation for politics or any human action and, hence, whether scientific authority can underwrite political authority. Given Weber's own preeminent authority as a social scientist in Germany at this time, this is not simply a question concerning the pedagogic ethics of those of his contemporaries—both left-wing and right-wing—who

---

[27] Seven months after delivering "Science as a Vocation," Weber presented a lecture entitled "Socialism" to officers of the Austro-Hungarian army in a political context characterized by fears of Socialist revolution in Central European states.

[28] See Peter Lassman and Irving Velody, eds., *Max Weber's "Science as a Vocation"* (London: Unwin Hyman, 1989) for a selection of the most important engagements with Weber's lecture by his contemporaries.

[29] Cited in Eduard Baumgarten, *Max Weber, Werk und Person* (Tübingen: Mohr, 1964), p. 554.

espoused a given political standpoint from the academic lectern, but also one of the relationship between Weber's own scholarly writings on political issues and his political writings as a citizen. If science cannot ground politics (as Weber resolutely concludes), this raises the second topic even more sharply: What is the meaning and value of scientific activity in the modern world? Just what is it that one is committed to, and bound by, in dedicating oneself to scientific work? It is in and through his engagements—at once passionate and sober—with these topics that Weber offers his account of science as a vocation in a lecture that is, simultaneously, a free-speaking meditation on the conditions, value, and limits of scientific work and an exemplary instance of such work.

Weber's lecture is composed in three movements: the external conditions of the vocation of science in the context of the increasing rationalization and bureaucratization of the university; the nature of the inner vocation for science given the (scientific) disenchantment of the world; and the role and value of the vocation of science for life under these fateful conditions of rationalization, bureaucratization, and disenchantment.

Each movement can be read as "making explicit" a given aspect of what it is to engage in scientific work under the conditions of our modern world and, simultaneously, as dispelling certain idols precisely by making explicit the forms of self-deception about the reality of our conditions that are presupposed in constituting these idols as idols. In this respect, Weber's lecture is concerned with cultivating the self-knowledge required by his audience if they are to acknowledge what is entailed by the commitment to scientific work. That this "clarity" is his aim is no accident since, as we will see, it is in the provision of such clarity concerning our possible stances toward and activities within the world that Weber locates the ethical value of scientific work.

It is important to note in this context that the word *Wissenschaft* carries with it a far broader reference than does the contemporary Anglo-Saxon term "science."[30] *Wissen* derives from Old Germanic words for wisdom, as opposed to "science," which derives from the Latin for knowledge.[31] *Wissenschaft* describes any organized body

---

[30] This paragraph is indebted to conversations with Professor Babette Babich and her forthcoming paper in a book edited by Gregory Moore and Thomas Brobjer on *Nietzsche and Science*.

[31] The first noted usages date back to the ninth century. It is worth nothing that among the meanings of "wise" is "song."

of knowledge the pursuit of which is social in the sense that it can be learned. Thus one can speak of studying *Kunstwissenschaft* rather than "art history" or *theologische Wissenschaft* rather than "theological studies." The German sense is best conveyed perhaps in an English expression like "she has it down to a science." Weber's lecture is addressed to all those who have disciplined or who would dedicate themselves to a particular area of knowledge.

1. THE EXTERNAL CONDITIONS OF SCIENCE AS A VOCATION

Weber's opening reflections on the external conditions of scientific work in Germany in 1917 have not typically received the attention that they deserve.[32] On the face of it, Weber is simply offering a brief comparison between the employment and working practices of German and American universities and their effects with respect to academic career prospects, together with the observation that German universities—and German life in general—are increasingly becoming "Americanized." It is tempting in this context to skim over this section in order to plunge that much more quickly into the excitingly "existential" reflections of the rest of the lecture, in which Weber's gift for dramatic oratory is given fuller expression. Certainly Weber is all too aware of the presence of this temptation in his audience. Following his reflections on the external conditions of scientific work, he offers this acknowledgment: "But I believe that you really wish to hear about something else, about an *inner* vocation for science" (S 7). Why, then, has Weber chosen to begin with what he describes himself as "a pedantic approach"?

To make clear the compelling reason that leads Weber to open with these reflections—and its direct relation to the idealistic temptation that he discerns in his audience—we need to recognize that his starting point is to acknowledge that a significant aspect of what it means to engage in scientific work (or to embark on a scientific career) is to work within a set of university institutions that are subject to the processes of rationalization and bureaucratization

---

[32] An important exception to this rule is Peter Lassman and Irving Velody's essay "Max Weber on Science, Disenchantment and the Search of Meaning" in Lassman and Velody, *Max Weber's "Science as a Vocation,"* pp. 159–204, which contains an excellent discussion of Weber's remarks on this topic. See also Wolfgang Schluchter, *Wertfreiheit und Verantwortungsethik: zum Verhältnis von Wissenschaft und Politik bei Max Weber* (Tübingen: Mohr, 1971).

characteristic of European cultural life at this time. The delineation of this fact is the point of his comparison of German and American universities, and it is a fact that has significant consequences for the fate of the individual scholar in Germany.[33]

Here Weber is responding to the reality of the slow but accelerating collapse of the Humboldtian vision of the university. In 1810 Wilhelm von Humboldt laid the basis for a university that would be oriented to research and teaching, funded from public coffers and committed to advancing the frontiers of knowledge for its own sake. In Humboldt's vision the university was to be free from interference from governmental authority. He called for *Freiheit der Lehre und des Lernens*—freedom of teaching and learning; indeed, it was the role of the government to promote freedom of research and teaching. To this extent the university was for all practical purposes to be self-governing and self-regulating.[34]

In Weber's understanding, this vision had been severely eroded, to the point of becoming effectively no more than the grin of the Cheshire cat. Weber's sketch of the consequences of this transformation begins by noting that it entails that the role of the university professor and of the assistant[35] are being reconfigured in managerial terms in the context of the development of the "state capitalist" character of university institutes (most obviously in the medical and natural sciences). A professor's position is increasing similar to that of a manager, while an assistant's situation is becoming markedly like that of a factory worker. This development is, in Weber's view, likely to become generalized across intellectual disciplines: "I am convinced that this development will continue to spread to disciplines like my own where the artisan is still the owner of his own resources (which amount essentially to the library), just as the old craftsman in the past owned the tools of his trade. This development

---

[33] Weber's concern with the condition of the German university and academic politics was an abiding one; thus it has been estimated that he wrote about twenty-five journalistic statements on this topic between 1908 and 1911. For an excellent discussion of this feature of Weber's work, see Wilhelm Hennis, "The Pitiless 'Sobriety of Judgment': Max Weber between Carl Menger and Gustav von Schmoller—the Academic Politics of Value Freedom," *History of the Human Sciences* 4, no. 1 (1991): 27–59.

[34] For an excellent short account see Herbert Schnädelbach, *Philosophy in Germany, 1831–1933* (Cambridge: Cambridge University Press, 1984), pp. 21–32.

[35] Although the U.S. terms assistant professor, associate professor, and professor have their origin in the German hierarchy, *Assistent* was then (and today even more so) much less prestigious than the corresponding American term.

is in full swing"(S 4). The moral of Weber's remarks has been appropriately drawn by Lassman and Velody:

> In this seemingly matter-of-fact way, Weber is here charting the decline in the position of the *Bildungsbürgertum* [the intellectual bourgeoisie] which is being undermined by a profound institutional transformation. . . . The Humboldtian ideal of the university has been overtaken by events and the idea of there being an intrinsic connection between science and culture is fast becoming an historical myth. In effect, Weber was, as he characteristically claimed, relentlessly stripping away the illusion that the modern university could be, if indeed it ever had been, an institution fashioned after the model propounded by Fichte and Humboldt.[36]

Thus, as Weber remarks: "Both in essence and appearance, the old *constitution* of the university has become a fiction" (S 4). However, Weber continues: "What has remained and has even been radically intensified is a feature peculiar to a university *career*. This is the fact that for a lecturer, let alone an assistant, to succeed in rising to the position of a full professor or even the head of an institute is purely a matter of *luck*. Chance is not the only factor, but its influence is quite exceptional" (S 4).

The central place of chance in the university career structure is, as Weber notes, partly due to the nature of academic selection practices, which, like professional selection practices in general, tend to select the second or third rather than "favorite" candidate (an issue that Weber takes to be of some scientific interest). However, this does not by itself account for the exceptionally large role of chance in academic life. Rather, explaining this exceptional feature of academic careers involves grasping that, under the actual conditions obtaining in German universities, the traditional ideal of the mutually supporting relationship of scholarship and teaching expressed in the personality of the lecturer is extrinsically problematic. Now Weber reminds us in passing that this ideal is also intrinsically problematic, because the ability to do significant research and the ability to teach well do not necessarily coincide: "A man can be both an outstanding scholar and an execrable teacher. I may remind you of the teaching activities of such men as Helmholtz or Ranke (S 5–6).[37]

---

[36] Lassman and Velody, "Max Weber on Science," 179.

[37] Hermann Helmholtz (1821–94) was one of the outstanding German scientists of the nineteenth century, notable for his contributions in both physics and physiology. His achievements include the formulation of the principle of the conservation of

But, Weber argues, it is the extrinsically problematic character of the traditional ideal under modern circumstances that accounts for the exceptional role of chance in academic careers. The traditional ideal is extrinsically problematic because it has given rise to a practice of appointing lecturers as both teachers and researchers, which, given the dissolution of the Humboldtian legitimation of scientific knowledge in terms of its cultural value, gives rise to a tendency to evaluate the lecturer in terms of the number of students attracted by his courses. Just as the politician must in the modern world compete for votes, so the lecturer must make himself attractive to students. As Weber puts it:

> [T]he number of enrolled students is a statistically tangible proof of success, whereas the qualities of a scholar are imponderable and frequently (and very naturally) a matter of dispute, particularly in the case of bold innovators.
>
> For this reason almost everyone succumbs to the idea that large student numbers are a blessing and a value in their own right. If a lecturer is said to be a bad teacher, this amounts in most cases to an academic death warrant, even if he is the greatest scholar in the world. But the question of whether an academic is a good teacher or a bad one is answered with reference to the frequency with which students honor him with their presence (S 6).

Yet, as Weber points out, "[I]t is also true that the fact that students flock to a teacher is determined largely by purely extraneous factors such as his personality or even his tone of voice—to a degree that might scarcely be thought possible" (S 6).

Thus, Weber concludes that "academic life is an utter gamble"— and it is with this conclusion that Weber's reason for beginning with this review of the external conditions of academic life becomes clear:

> When young students come to me to seek advice about qualifying as a lecturer, the responsibility of giving it is scarcely to be borne. Of course, if the student is a Jew, you can only say: *lasciate ogni speranza*.[38] But others, too, must be asked to examine their conscience: Do you believe that you can bear to see one mediocrity after another being promoted over your head year after year, without your

---

energy. Leopold von Ranke (1795–1886) was a leading German historian whose search for historical objectivity greatly influenced historiography throughout Europe. Both had chairs in Berlin.

[38] "Abandon all hope." Dante places these words over the entrance to Hell, in the *Inferno*. The sign continues with "*voi ch'entrate*" ("ye who enter here").

becoming embittered and warped? Needless to say, you always receive the same answer: of course, I live only for my "vocation"— but I, at least, have found only a handful of people who have survived this process without injury to their personality. (S 7)

Weber concludes: "So much for the external conditions of a scholarly vocation."

In other words, the idealistic temptation that Weber discerns in his audience, the desire to focus on the inner vocation for science rather than on its external conditions, is just that temptation which reveals itself and its effects in the all-too-easy answer "Naturally, I live only for my 'vocation.'" By starting his lecture in a "pedantic" spirit of matter-of-factness, Weber is seeking to sober up his audience, to cultivate a certain pathos of distance in them, by demonstrating the potentially tragic consequences of failing to acknowledge the real conditions of scientific work in the modern university. To attend only to the inner dimension of science as a vocation, on Weber's account, is to increase one's vulnerability to the damage that the role of chance in academic life can engender. It is so precisely because the failure to recognize that one is exposed to luck in this way makes one liable to construe instances of this fate not as immanent features of the modern academic career but as examples of intentional injustice on the part of some agent (say, the university). Consequently, if one's luck is bad, one is liable to be increasingly consumed by feelings of resentment toward the agent or agents that one holds responsible for one's victimhood, and this twisting of one's soul in bitterness is a form of damage that the acknowledgment of the real conditions of academic life could have helped one to avoid or, at the very least, mitigate. In making plain the character of an academic career in the modern university, Weber is enjoining his audience to acknowledge the conditions that will ineluctably govern their professional lives if they embark on such a career.

2. THE COMMITMENT TO SCIENCE

Having sobered up his audience, Weber turns to the more obviously intoxicating issue of the contemporary meaning of science as a vocation; it is worth noting, however, that in doing so, Weber immediately proposes a highly demanding account of what commitment to this vocation entails. Continuing his concern with external constraints on science as vocation, Weber begins by stressing that, today, scientific activity is necessarily specialized in character and hence requires a certain capacity for self-restriction on the part of the scholar. Suddenly shifting into an Old Testament tone of almost prophetic fervor, he proclaims:

> And anyone who lacks the ability to don blinkers for once and to convince himself that the destiny of his soul depends upon whether he is right to make precisely this conjecture and no other at this point in his manuscript should keep well away from science. He will never be able to submit to what we may call the "experience" of science. In the absence of this strange intoxication that outsiders greet with a pitying smile, without this passion, this conviction that "millennia had to pass before you were born, and millennia more must wait in silence" to see if your conjecture will be confirmed—without this you do *not* possess this vocation for science and should turn your hand to something else. For nothing has any value for a human being as a human being unless he *can* pursue it with *passion*. (S 8)

So Weber sets the bar high: it is the fate of one's soul that is at stake. And we can see why, for it is only individuals who are capable of undergoing this "experience" of science who will be able to draw on this experience, on such epiphanic moments of frenzy, in resisting the force of (and hence overcoming) the exposure to feelings of *ressentiment* that Weber has already located as an almost inevitable feature of academic careers in the modern university. In one's undertaking of the "experience" of science, Weber is suggesting, one finds the ethical resources to resist being consumed by the feelings of *ressentiment* that naturally arise from seeing mediocrity promoted over one's head year after year. Note, though, that at a mundane level, this necessary epiphany consists in caring passionately about footnotes, as it were, and in specializing one's work. The above paragraph is not in praise of the generalist but of the specialist, whose speciality is in a deep sense his or her *own* specialty.

However, while such passion is a necessary condition of having a vocation for science, it is not a sufficient condition. On the contrary, entitlement to the claim that one possesses a vocation for science depends on one's commitment to two further conditions. The first of these commitments is to the necessity of working diligently while acknowledging that work, even combined with passion, cannot guarantee the generation of significant ideas. As Weber puts it:

> And for its part, work cannot replace inspiration or force it to appear, any more than passion can. Both work and passion, and

especially both *together*, can entice an idea. Ideas come in their own good time, not when we want them. . . . At any rate, ideas come when they are least expected, rather than while you are racking your brains at your desk. But by the same token, they would not have made their appearance if we had not spent many hours pondering at our desks or brooding passionately over the problems facing us.

However that may be, the scholar must resign himself to the element of chance that is involved in every kind of scientific endeavor. It is expressed in the question: Will inspiration come or not? A man may be an outstanding worker[39] and yet never have had a valuable idea of his own. (S 9)

Given this immanent risk of scientific work, we can see once again why Weber stresses the importance of passion for science; such passion provides resources not only for coping with bad luck with respect to the extrinsic risks of the profession of science but also with bad luck in relation to its intrinsic risks. The second of the additional commitments required is specified by Weber in terms of *personality*, having an idea of one's *own*. By "personality"—being one's own self—he refers to the subordination of oneself to the values and norms of one's vocation: "[I]n the realm of science, the only person to have 'personality' is the one who is *wholly devoted to his subject*. And this is true not just of science" (S 10). This appeal to the idea of personality, an idea that plays a significant role in Weber's thought more generally,[40] plays two related roles in this context.

First, it makes clear to his audience Weber's opposition to the "life as art" movement in late Wilhelmian and then later in Weimar culture, a movement associated with figures such as Stefan George valorizing *personal experience* as pure individuality guided by the idea of making oneself a work of art. Weber pours scorn on the cult of the idol of personal experience both generally (allowing a possible exception only for figures such as Goethe, who came along "once in a thousand years," and even then suggesting that such figures pay a

---

[39] To drive home the point about the proletarianization of the intellectual world, Weber refers to the intellectual as a "worker" four times in the essay.

[40] In *Roscher and Knies: The Logical Problems of Historical Economics* (New York: Free Press, 1975), Weber specifies the concept of personality as "a constant and intrinsic relation to certain ultimate 'values' and 'meanings' of life" (p. 192). For consideration of Weber's use of this concept, see Ralph Schroeder, "'Personality' and 'Inner Distance': The Conception of the Individual in Max Weber's Sociology," *History of the Human Sciences* 4, no. 1 (1991): 61–78.

significant price for such a project) and particularly in relation to scientific work:

> [I]n the realm of science, however, we may say categorically that if a man appears on the stage as the impresario of the subject to which he devotes himself and if he attempts to legitimate himself by appealing to his "personal experience," this is not enough to turn him into a personality. Nor is it the sign of a personality to go on to ask: How can I show that I am more than just a mere "expert"? How can I manage to prove that I can say something in form or substance, that no one has ever said? This phenomenon has increased massively nowadays and always seems petty. It always diminishes the man who asks such questions instead of allowing his inner dedication to his task and to it alone to raise him to the height and the dignity of the cause he purports to serve. (S 10–11)

This is the case, Weber argues, in both science and art. But while in both cases personality requires the subordination of the self to the needs of the subject, the distinct natures of artistic and scientific work entail that the content of such personality in these fields is quite distinct—and this brings us to Weber's second point, namely, that whereas the artist can aspire to produce a work that is never surpassed, this is not the case with the scientist, whose work is destined precisely to be surpassed. Returning once more to the language of fate, Weber writes:

> A work of art that truly achieves "fulfillment" will never be surpassed; it will never grow old. The individual can assess its significance for himself personally in different ways. But no one will ever be able to say that a work that achieves genuine "fulfillment" in an artistic sense has been "superseded" by another work that likewise achieves "fulfillment."
>
> Contrast that with the realm of science, where we all know that what we have achieved will be obsolete in ten, twenty, or fifty years. That is the fate, indeed, that is the very *meaning* of scientific work. It is subject to and dedicated to this meaning in quite a specific sense, in contrast to every other element of culture of which the same might be said in general. Every scientific "fulfillment" gives birth to new "questions" and *cries out* to be surpassed and rendered obsolete. Everyone who wishes to serve science has to resign himself to this. The products of science can undoubtedly remain important for a long time, as "objects of pleasure" because of their artistic qualities, or as a means of training others in scientific work. But we must repeat: to be superseded scientifically is not simply our fate but our goal. We cannot work without living in hope that others will advance beyond us. (S 11)

Science is not art and can never endure: to live for science means never to accomplish anything of lasting value.[41] Weber's vision of the scientific enterprise here thus relates it, on the one hand, to what Marx saw as characteristic of capitalism—that commodities were produced only to be exchanged and not for use—and, on the other, to Nietzsche's analysis of the possibility of truth—that nothing in the way one pursued truth could possibly lead something to count as finally and definitively true.

Weber must therefore seek other motives or qualities that make science possible. He argues that to be entitled to claim that one has a vocation for science requires passion, diligence combined with the acknowledgment of the role of luck in intellectual activity, and personality, where the content of scientific personality requires acknowledgment precisely that it is the fate of science to be subject to progress such that one's work becomes obsolete. These are demanding criteria, but, in addition, the last of these criteria poses a very particular worry in Weber's view. He formulates this concern as follows: "In principle, this progress is infinite. This brings us to the *problem of the meaning* of science. For it is far from self-evident that a thing that is subject to such a law can itself be meaningful and rational. What is the point of engaging in something that neither comes, nor can come, to an end in reality?" (S 11–2).[42]

This worry is pressing for Weber, and he devotes the remainder of the essay to consideration of possible responses. Weber, it should also be said, found this personally problematic. After delivering the "Science" lecture, he found himself in conversation with his young friend Karl Jaspers and the Berlin jurist Richard Thoma. In replying to Thoma, who held that the message of the lecture entailed that Weber knew neither what scholarship meant nor why he engaged in it, Jaspers reports that Weber, "wounded visibly," said: "Well, if you

---

[41] Though it cannot be explored here, this is also the theme that underlies Nietzsche's *The Birth of Tragedy*, a theme that Nietzsche makes evident in the 1886 "Attempt at a Self-critique" that he adds to the second edition.

[42] Though Weber could not have known it here, the existence of the possibility of the destruction of the human species consequent to nuclear warfare poses a new problem for his position, which assumes that there *will be* a future, even if the worth of each individual act is undone. On this, see George Kateb, "Thinking about Human Extinction: (I) Nietzsche and Heidegger," *Raritan* 2 (Fall 1986): 1–28, and "Thinking about Human Extinction: (II) Emerson and Whitman," *Raritan* 3 (Winter 1987): 1–22, as well as Reinhard Bendix, "An Exchange of Letters between the Author and a Graduate Student," in *Force, Fate, and Freedom: On Historical Sociology* (Berkeley and Los Angeles: University of California Press, 1984).

insist: to see what one can bear, but it is better not to talk of such things."[43] His response recalls, perhaps purposively, Nietzsche's apothegm about "strength of spirit" that appears in the epigraph to this Introduction.

3. THE DISENCHANTMENT OF THE WORLD

Weber's starting point for his reflection on the problem of the meaning and value of science begins by acknowledging that scientific progress is "the most important fraction" of the process of intellectual rationalization, which he refers to as "the disenchantment of the world." This process of disenchantment raises a question that Weber finds expressed in its purest form by Tolstoy, namely, whether death (and hence life) is a meaningful occurrence for modern people. Tolstoy's response is that it is not, precisely because the occurrence of death marks a moment not of final completion, in which one is satiated with life, but of depletion, in which one is tired of life. Be this as it may (and Weber will return to consideration of Tolstoy later), Weber's immediate concern is not with this general question but with the more specific issue of science as a vocation: "What is the *vocation of science* within the totality of human life and what is its value?"

At this stage, Weber briefly considers the ways in which the value of science has been grounded in the past. His survey takes us from science as a way to true being (Plato), as a way to true art (Leonardo), as a way to true nature (Francis Bacon), as a way to the true God (the Pietist Swammerdam), and as a way to true happiness (which he attributes with Nietzschean nastiness to "some overgrown children among the professoriat or in editorial offices"). However, he argues, all of these previous grounds for valuing science are illusions to which we can no longer cling—and so the pressing question returns: What is the meaning and value of science? Following Nietzsche's argument that there is no such thing as a science without presuppositions,[44] Weber acknowledges the central difficulty that this question

---

[43] *Hannah Arendt/Karl Jaspers Correspondence* 1926–1969. Edited by Lotte Kohler and Hans Saner. Translated by Robert and Rita Kimber (New York: Harcourt Brace Jovanovich, 1992). Jaspers to Arendt, pp. 660–1; see also 661–2.

[44] The best and most extensive study of Nietzsche's understanding of science is Babette E. Babich, *Nietzsche's Philosophy of Science: Reflecting Science on the Ground of Art and Life* (Albany: SUNY Press, 1994). See also Robin Small, *Nietzsche in Context* (Aldershot, Eng.: Ashgate, 2001), for a study of Nietzsche's knowledge of and relation to nineteenth-century science, as well as Gregory Moore, *Nietzsche, Biology, and Metaphor* (Cambridge: Cambridge University Press, 2002).

poses: science presupposes that what is produced by scientific work is worth knowing, but it cannot itself ground this presupposition; it cannot tell us why scientific knowledge is worth knowing because it cannot address questions of value. Weber comments:

> The simplest reply was given by Tolstoy with his statement, "Science is meaningless because it has no answer to the only questions that matter to us: 'What should we do? How shall we live?'" The fact that science cannot give us this answer is absolutely indisputable. The question is only in what sense does it give "no" answer, and whether or not it might after all prove useful for somebody who is able to ask the right question. (S 17)

Before considering how, for Weber, there might be a valuable sense in which science gives us "no" answer, it is worth noting that the claim that science cannot address questions of value grounds Weber's argument that science cannot ground politics (as Marx had hoped) and, more particularly, that intellectual integrity demands that lecturers not expound their own political views in the lecture hall. To have a vocation for science thus involves this further commitment in just the sense that to espouse a political position from the lectern is a betrayal of the intellectual demands of one's subject; it is to make a claim that cannot be scientifically grounded and yet is presented under the auspices of one's authority as a scientist.

Is there, then, a sense in which science can give us "no" answer to the question of how one should live that grounds the meaning and value of *science?* If not, it would seem that to commit oneself to science as a vocation is simply irrational. However, Weber argues that there is just such a sense and that science does have an important ethical role to play within the totality of human life, namely, to provide *clarity* concerning "ultimate" problems:

> This brings us to the last contribution that science can make in the service of clarity, and at the same time we reach its limits. We can and should tell you that the *meaning* of this or that practical stance can be inferred consistently, and hence also honestly, from this or that ultimate fundamental ideological position. It may be deducible from one position, or from a number—but there are other quite specific philosophies from which it cannot be inferred. To put it metaphorically, if you choose this particular standpoint, you will be serving this particular god and will *give offense to every other god.* For you will necessarily arrive at such-and-such ultimate, internally meaningful *conclusions* if you remain true to yourselves. We may assert this at least in principle. The discipline of philosophy and the

discussion of what are ultimately the philosophical bases of the individual disciplines all attempt to achieve this. If we understand the matter correctly (something that must be assumed here) we can compel a person, or at least help him, *to render an account of the ultimate meaning of his own actions.* (S 26)

In enforcing clarity, science enforces upon you the presuppositions that make possible the activity you have undertaken. Weber takes this very radically. Thus not only is a doctor *in the vocation of doctor* unquestioningly committed to health as a value, and a lawyer in the terms of his or her vocation to the constitutive value of the existence of law as that which permits him to do and be what he is, but this is also true in science. Thus "Kant's epistemology . . . proceeded from the assumption that 'scientific truth exists and it is *valid*' and then went on to inquire what intellectual assumptions are required for this to be (meaningfully) possible" (S 28–9). Note that for Weber the very concept of (scientific) truth is a constitutive assumption necessary for the practice of science and no more.

If it is to perform this role of clarification, science must operate against the background assumption that there is a plurality of incompatible orientations to life. While nowadays this Nietzschean claim might seem hardly controversial, at least in its milder versions, it is important to understand that Weber insists that it holds for science, including his own. Moreover, if we are concerned to seek an example of science playing this ethical role, we need look no further than the lecture "Science as a Vocation" itself—for here Weber has been concerned precisely with making explicit what is involved in an ultimate orientation to truth in one's professional life and clarifying the circumstances and commitments involved in acting on the basis of this ultimate orientation in a way that is designed precisely to create "a sense of duty, clarity, and a feeling of responsibility."

4. A Meaning for Life?

There is, however, a final issue concerning Weber's lecture that requires clarification, and here, in a sense, we return to Tolstoy's challenge concerning the meaning of life under conditions of disenchantment. This issue concerns Weber's invocation of the language of fate and his insistence on the virtue of intellectual integrity, that is, of being prepared to acknowledge the character of the modern world in which one is situated and the commitments that this imposes on us. Although Weber has invoked Nietzsche's thought both explicitly (with respect to the critique of science as a way to happiness) and implicitly (with regard to the impossibility of science without presuppositions), it is in his confrontation with Tolstoy's challenge that Weber's commitment to Nietzsche's diagnosis of, and prescription for, our modern malaise is most prominent.[45]

The first point to note is that Weber's view that the turn to religion under modern conditions involves a "sacrifice of intellect" and his commitment to a "polytheism" of ultimate orientations to life simply expresses his acknowledgment of Nietzsche's account of the death of God. Against this background, Weber's stress on the importance of intellectual integrity should be seen as an endorsement of Nietzsche's claim that honesty expressed as intellectual probity is the preeminently necessary modern virtue[46]—and the pathos with which Weber invests this virtue, namely, that it is our very truthfulness that deprives us of the illusions (for example, illusions concerning the meaning and value of science) from which we might otherwise draw comfort, precisely echoes Nietzsche's own recognition that it is the commitment to truthfulness cultivated under the aegis of Christianity (or, more strictly, the ascetic ideal) that undermines Christianity. In this context Nietzsche's response was to argue that any post-Christian ethics must be structured around a commitment to *amor fati,* the love of fate. Our lives have ethical meaning, by this account, insofar as we acknowledge and affirm our fate, that is, the circumstances and commitments of our agency, as the condition of our agency and, more particularly, of the meaning and value of our agency. In other words, Tolstoy's challenge can

---

[45] Weber's relationship to Nietzsche has been sketched well by Wilhelm Hennis' *Max Weber: Essays in Reconstruction* (London: Unwin Hyman, 1998) and examined extensively in Robert Eden, *Political Leadership and Nihilism: A Study of Weber and Nietzsche* (Gainesville: University Press of Florida, 1983). It has been further explored in a number of recent articles; see David Owen, "'Autonomy' and 'Inner Distance': A Trace of Nietzsche in Weber," *History of the Human Sciences* 4, no. 1 (1991): 79–91, and "Of Overgrown Children and Last Men: Nietzsche's Critique and Max Weber's Cultural Science," *Nietzsche-Studien* 29 (2000): 252–66; Ralph Schroeder, "Nietzsche and Weber: Two Prophets of the Modern Age," in Scott Lash and Sam Whimster, eds., *Max Weber, Rationality and Modernity* (London: Unwin, 1987); Tracy B. Strong, "What Have We to Do with Morals? Nietzsche and Weber on History and Ethics," *History of the Human Sciences* 5, no. 3 (1992): 9–18, and "Love, Passion, and Maturity: Nietzsche and Weber on Morality and Politics," in John McCormick, ed., *Democracy and Technology* (Durham, NC: Duke University Press, 2002).

[46] See, for example, Nietzsche's *The Gay Science,* ed. Bernard Williams (Cambridge: Cambridge University Press, 2001), p. 335.

be met to the extent that we acknowledge and affirm the fateful character of our lives.

How, though, does this Nietzschean response to Tolstoy relate to Weber's reflection on science as a vocation? The relationship is this: in "Science as a Vocation" Weber is, carefully and precisely, specifying the fateful character of scientific activity and commitment to that activity. In other words, Weber is specifying the conditions of "love of scientific fate" in all its difficulty. From this Nietzschean perspective, Weber's concern with what it is to have a vocation for science is a concern with what it is to love one's fate as a scientist, that is, to embrace our condition of being thrown into the world as it is.

ON "POLITICS AS A VOCATION"

If the "Science" lecture was delivered under conditions of war weariness, the "Politics" lecture was held, also in Munich, on January 28, 1919, in a context of high political drama. Like the "Science" lecture, it is a "philosophical" text in that it seeks to elaborate on the nature of politics and of human action in modern times, but it is also a lecture given under particular circumstances at a particular place. Most centrally, what had happened since the "Science" lecture was Germany's defeat. The war that came to be known as World War I had been originally thought a minor skirmish with a probable duration of less than a year. As it had dragged on into its fourth year and unprecedented casualties, opinion in Germany had polarized between those nationalists who wished to prosecute the fighting fully and various groups of a more or less thoroughly pacifist orientation who wished to bring it to an end. To general surprise, the end had come sooner rather than later, and Germany had surrendered on November 11, 1918, without any widespread sense that it had been in any way at fault. On November 23, 1918, the parliamentary Socialist intellectual Kurt Eisner had released a set of official documents that cast doubt on the purity of Germany's intentions in 1914.[47] Weber, whose sympathies were in support of German honor (and thus against any insistence on a confession of

---

[47] For a complete discussion of this and the release by the Spartacist League of a memorandum by Lichnowsky, see Allan Mitchell, *Revolution in Bavaria, 1918–1919: The Eisner Regime and the Soviet Republic* (Princeton, NJ: Princeton University Press, 1965).

German guilt for the origins of the war) and in defense of the German national interest, had raised the possibility of a mass mobilization of the German people in defense of the fatherland.[48] In addition, in a set of newspaper articles Weber had given and continued to give considerable time to the development and public expression of the institutions that he thought might best preserve the German nation.[49]

For both pacifists and nationalists, however, the defeat of Germany came as an unexpected shock. In Bavaria Eisner was elected prime minister in early November 1918. Many of those involved in his government were friends of Weber from many years back. With the development of Councils of Workers and Soldiers (modeled to some degree on Lenin's proposals and analyses in *State and Revolution*), the new government shuddered rapidly and somewhat chaotically to the left.

It is in the midst of these developments that Weber gave the "Politics" lecture. He had, as discussed above, given the lecture on *Wissenschaft* some fourteen months earlier. Weber had at first refused the request of Immanuel Birnbaum, rector of the University of Munich, to give a second lecture, but when, in the fall of 1918 Birnbaum indicated that he would ask Eisner instead, Weber relented. Weber continued to resist the invitation, however, suggesting as late as early January 1919 that his friend Friedrich Naumann—"a representative German politician"—replace him. Two other events intervened: Naumann fell sick and would have been unable to give the lecture, and on January 15 the Spartacists[50] Karl Liebknecht and Rosa Luxemburg, who had played important roles in the Bavarian soviet and had initiated a left-wing uprising in early January in Berlin, were assassinated. Weber, despite his misgivings, agreed to give the lecture.[51]

---

[48] See the discussion in Sam Whimster, ed., *Max Weber and the Culture of Anarchy* (New York: St. Martin's Press, 1999), especially the articles by Carl Levy and Karl-Ludwig Ay, pp. 83–128. See also Marianne Weber, *Max Weber: A Biography*.

[49] See, for instance, "The President of the Reich" and "Parliament and Government in Germany under a New Political Order," in PW. See his letter to Helene Weber, November 18, 1918, and the letter to Friederich Crusius, the same day. Letters are cited from the volumes published in the *Gesamtausgabe* (see Texts of Weber in German).

[50] The Spartacist League was the ancestor of the German Communist Party.

[51] He wrote to Else Jaffe on January 23, 1919, that "The lecture on the 28th will be poor, for I will have very much something else in my head than the 'vocation' of a 'politician.'"

It was again important to Weber that the talk was to be given as part of the series instigated by the Freistudentische Bund—the group that he hoped might become a bridge between the universities and the German population at large, one that might enhance the political education and maturity of the nation.[52] It is only *after* Weber's lecture, when popular elections were eventually called in which the majority Socialists won a resounding victory, that, on his way to resign as prime minister, Kurt Eisner was assassinated by the proto-fascist Count Arco-Valley. The Bavarian soviet and the Spartacist uprising were shortly to be savagely repressed.

The war had intensified what Weber thought to be the characteristic of his age: the desire for certainty, that is, the desire to give some secure definition to human circumstances. For Weber, such desire was dangerous, for if, as he believed, human affairs were never finally fixed, the wish that they would be would inevitably lead to disappointment and resentment. In the middle of November 1918, shortly after the defeat, he wrote to Else Jaffe: "And I fear, when it seems that faith can indeed overturn mountains but not clean up ruined finances and a lack of capital—that then after all that men have already undergone, the frustration[53] will in fact not be supportable by many of the faithful, and they will be spiritually [*innerlich*] bankrupt."[54] The hard facts of the situation—finances and capital—will, in Weber's reading, destroy those who thought that the world might be made new.

The lecture was thus given not only in a political hothouse and a seriously underdefined political situation but also under circumstances that threatened the integrity and identity of human beings. On the one hand, it was simply not clear what the future of the Bavarian regime would be, nor was the status of defeated Germany clear. As the war had dragged on, it had changed character. With the Soviet Revolution and the entry of the United States into the fray, both in 1917, victory had increasingly come to be seen as requiring a moral justification. The suffering and death had been too great to be

---

[52] For more details and references on the student league see the "Editorial Report" in Max Weber, *Gesamtausgabe I/17, Wissenschaft als Beruf/Politik als Beruf,* Wolfgang Mommsen and Wolfgang Schluchter, eds. (Tübingen: Mohr, 1991), pp. 50 ff.

[53] The German is *Enttäuschung.* See the discussion of the translation of this term immediately below.

[54] "Und ich fürchte, wenn sich zeigt, daß Glaube zwar Berge versetzen aber nicht ruinierte Finanzen und Kapitalmangel sanieren kann, wird die Enttäuschung—nach allem, was dem Menschen sonst schon genommen ist, für viele gerade der Gläubigsten unerträglich werden und sie innerlich bankerott machen" (GPS 481).

justified simply by victory—moral right, the good of humanity, had to triumph.[55] In this context, it is worth noting that Weber will later accompany the German delegation to Versailles and pronounce the terms demanded of Germany "shameful" in that they placed the moral onus on Germany.[56]

If the moralization of the war is threatening to Germany as a nation, the defeat also threatens the identity of his compatriots and his audience. Weber fears that it will lead them in the future to increasingly dangerous attitudes toward, and expectations of, politics. The "Science" lecture had opened with his assertion that he spoke in response to the demands of the audience. He had begun by placing the vocation of science in a web of "pedantry." Here again his opening words—the salutation to the audience, so to speak—are important: "The lecture I shall give in response to your wishes will necessarily frustrate you in a number of ways" (P 32).

A number of points should be noted. First, the *need* for the lecture comes from the audience: it is they who have asked Weber. Weber displays a notable reluctance to address this group, at this time, on this issue; indeed, as remarked above, he had not wanted to give this talk. Thus he is responding to a lack in his audience, a lack that will become one of the themes of his presentation. What they are missing, as we shall see, is any sense of what political maturity in the present or any foreseeable situation might be.

Second, the German word that has been translated here as "frustrate" is *enttäuschen,* a word that carries the meaning of both "disappoint" and "disillusion." What Weber has to say to the assembly will not only not provide them with what they think they need but at the same time take away the illusions under which they labor, not the least of which is wanting or hoping that a favorable resolution of the current situation might be found. His first move is both to distance the audience from any expectation that he will have answers for them and to give them enough distance from themselves so that they may think critically about themselves.

Thus, third, the frustration will be inevitable, because, as Weber goes on to say, his audience wants him to tell them what to do. This was in some sense to be expected: as noted above, Weber was at this

[55] See Arno Mayer, *Political Origins of the New Diplomacy, 1917–1918* (New Haven, CT: Yale University Press, 1959).

[56] See his essay "On the Theme of War Guilt" in GPS 381 ff.; see also his letter to the *Frankfurter Zeitung,* March 20, 1919, on the establishment of a commission to examine the question of war guilt (GPS 487).

time the most respected intellectual voice in Germany; his newspaper columns analyzing the contemporary and possible postwar political situations were models of clarity and decisiveness. From whom else, if not from him, might a disoriented Germany expect to have an answer? Weber's position, however, is that there is nothing to be done that his audience can be told. Solutions to the present situation will not come like pharmaceutical remedies: instead, a much longer treatment will be necessary.

1. The Internal Conditions of Political Vocation

Weber's opening sentence sets the stage, as it were, for the overall message of the lecture. As with the "Science" lecture, this lecture is also in several movements. Weber will again set out the conditions, both internal and external, that will have to be met for someone to face up to the demands of the times—here, the demands of political action—like an adult. In our considerations here, however, instead of proceeding, as does the lecture, from the external conditions to the internal ones, we shall take the reverse approach and start with a consideration of the internal qualities of the person who has politics as a vocation. We do this in order to dramatize by juxtaposition the degree to which the understanding of the person of vocation is the same in both lectures.[57]

Weber's last challenge in this lecture is similar to his challenge that had opened the "Science" lecture. It is to pose a question to whomever would partake of the political vocation as to whether he is "certain that his spirit will not be broken if the world, when looked at from his point of view, proves too stupid or base to accept what he wishes to offer it, and . . . when faced with all that obduracy, can still say 'Nevertheless!' despite everything" (P 93). He again confronts each member of the audience with a demand: can he or she pass a certain test, meet certain criteria, such that they are able to say "Nevertheless?" He had just previously warned his audience that most people will answer this question dishonestly or unthinkingly. The warning continues:

> We can only say one thing. We live in an age of excitement, which you may think is *not* of a "sterile" kind, though excitement is one thing, and it is not by any means always the same as authentic passion. Now

---

[57] Some portions of what follow have appeared in substantially different form in Strong, "Max Weber and the Bourgeoisie."

in such an age, conviction politicians may well spring up in large numbers *all of a sudden* and run riot, declaring, "The world is stupid and nasty, not I. The responsibility for the consequences cannot be laid at my door but must rest with those who employ me and whose stupidity or nastiness I shall do away with." And if this happens, I shall say openly that I would begin by asking how much *inner gravity* lies behind this ethics of conviction, and I suspect I should come to the conclusion that in nine cases out of ten I was dealing with windbags who do not genuinely feel what they are taking on themselves but who are making themselves drunk on romantic sensations." (P 92)

A distinction between those who are unable to face reality as it is because of their needs and desires and those who can come face to face with an indifferent world and maintain their selfhood—in this case, their vocation for politics—intact thus frames the lecture. What does one have to acknowledge for one to be able to participate in the political realm without self-delusion and self-destruction? The situation is fraught with dangers. Whoever becomes involved with politics, that is to say, with power and violence as a means, "has made a pact with satanic powers . . . [which are] inexorable and create consequences for their actions and also subjectively for themselves, against which they are helpless if they fail to perceive them"(P 91). The passage is key to understanding that Weber's purpose is not to legitimate what has come to be called *Realpolitik*—politics as the pursuit of power for its own sake. The overall purpose of the lecture is to provide a sketch of the political education necessary so that one might know what it is to move from the status of (much of) the audience to that of authentically having politics as one's vocation. Power is the necessary instrument but never the point of politics. But Weber makes clear in both lectures that to use power to is play with the devil and risk always the Faustian loss of one's soul.[58]

For Weber, this risk takes place in the context of historical processes that place demands on a nation to be ignored only at one's peril. In 1916, analyzing the position of Germany as a European world power, he can assert that Germany has *no choice* but to play a lead role in European and world political affairs. Why so? "Not out of pride, but out of our responsibility before history. Posterity will not ask for an account of the shaping of the culture of the earth from the Swiss, or the Danes, or the Dutch or the Norwegians." It is to Germany, he goes on to say, to live up to the "duty" of a state of

---

[58] See, for example, S 27 and P 91; in each text the same passage from *Faust* about the devil being old is cited.

seventy million inhabitants to be a "major power" (*Machtstaat*) and
to provide to the world an alternative other than "Anglo-Saxon convention and Russian bureaucracy." Indeed "the honor of [German]
national character demands it."[59] This vision is not simply a kind of
jingoism: indeed, it is the opposite. It asserts that whether Germany
wills it or not, its position in the world will inevitably mean that
whatever it does, it will have a major effect on the world. As in the
"Science" lecture, the historical context sets the terms of our fate and
cannot be avoided. Even if Germany were to choose "not" to play a
major role, this choice will itself have major consequences. Thus it
must accept its own role and determine in the context of that historical givenness precisely what it will (responsibly) do.[60] One might thus
think of this lecture as given with Lenin's famous 1902 text "What is
to be done?" in mind.[61] And whatever one took Lenin's answer to
be[62]—it is normally thought to be a call to action—Weber clearly did
not recommend any particular course. Indeed, much of the essay
explicitly counsels against thinking that there is a "solution."

2. Responsibility and Maturity

Why, however, does Weber eschew the chance to tell his audience
what must be done? The usual answer has been that Weber thought
it central to his vocation to keep separate the realms of values and
science. According to this understanding, one can never deduce facts

---

[59] "Deutschland unter den europäischen Weltmächten," GPS 91–2. We cannot but
help hearing in this something like the role that Tocqueville sees for Europe at the
end of *Democracy in America* (where he sees the bipolarity of America and Russia
as the structure of the coming world) and that Heidegger reserves for Germany and
Europe in *An Introduction to Metaphysics*.

[60] There are thus interesting parallels—worthy of investigation—between Weber's
position and that taken by Maurice Merleau-Ponty in *Humanism and Terror* (Boston, MA: Beacon, 1967).

[61] We do not know of a reference in Weber's corpus to this essay by Lenin. Weber
was, however, well aware of Lenin and had followed his disputes with Plekhanov
and others in relation to the editing of *Iskra* with considerable care. See "Zur Lage
der bürgerlichen Demokratie in Russland," GPS 53 and note 42a.

[62] In fact, Lenin's answer, as is not generally remembered, to the question of what is
to be done is "abolish the third stage," by which he means that the party should
become fully mature. The third stage is that of adolescence. For an analysis of the
parallels, see Tracy B. Strong, "Entitlement and Legitimacy: Weber and Lenin on
the Problems of Leadership," in Fred Eidlin, ed., *Constitutional Government and
Democracy: Festschrift for Henry Ehrmann* (New York: Westview Press, 1983).

from values nor values from facts.[63] Thus, still with this view, Weber, who explicitly appears before his audience as a political economist, that is, as a scholar, could not, in that role, for epistemological reasons exhort his audience to adopt a particular political position, for values are not, in this positivist reading, the subject of true knowledge. And indeed, throughout the lecture he disparages those academics—be they on the left or the right—who, like Dietrich Schäfer, did urge their listeners to take up a particular political stance.

There is some truth to this reading, but in the end it does not hold. Weber has concerns here that go far beyond the supposed irreducibility of the fact-value distinction. He sets out two kinds of attitudes. One he calls the "ethic of responsibility," the other the "ethic of conviction." An ethic of responsibility pays attention only to the actual consequences of what is done. To argue for responsibility is to require the acknowledgment that the consequences of a given action are one's own, no matter whether or not one intended them. Thus, famously, in an exchange with General Ludendorff after Germany's defeat in World War I, Weber asked him to take the blame publicly for the war on the grounds that he was in command. (Ludendorff would have none of it.)[64] This is contrasted with the ethic of "conviction."[65] The distinction between the two ethics has to do with the complete absence of intentionality as an excuse in the ethics of responsibility and its overdetermination of judgment in the ethics of conviction. Put more crudely, it does no good in politics to say that you did not intend the (unfortunate) consequences of your action. Anyone who does so, says Weber, is a "political infant."[66] Weber thus will refuse the relevance to politics of any deontological ethic, any ethic based on intentionality alone. If his epistemology is a radicalization of the Kantian critique, he sets himself here in opposition to what are generally regarded as "Kantian" ethics.[67]

---

[63] See the analysis in Tracy B. Strong, "History and Choices: The Political Thought of Raymond Aron," *History and Theory* 11, no. 2 (1972).

[64] See the transcript of the exchange in Hans Gerth and C. W. Mills' introduction to *From Max Weber* (New York: Oxford University Press, 1961), pp. 41–2.

[65] See below, P 83 f.

[66] For a comparison on Weber and Lenin on maturity and childhood, see Strong, "Entitlement and Legitimacy."

[67] We say "generally" as there is considerable scholarship that shows that understanding Kantian ethics as simply deontological is not accurate (nor does Weber say that it is). See the work of Dieter Henrich, Jerome Schneewind, Barbara Herman, Rolf-Peter Horstmann, and many others.

The matter, though, is not so simple as a straightforward binary opposition. While the two ethics are conceptually distinct, they can be (and under certain conditions for Weber *should* be) existentially linked. If it is wrong to believe in the privileging of one's subjective intentions for politics, it is also the case that an ethic resting on subjectivity and one resting on consequences can come together. When they do, they will have as their existential correlative the individual whom Weber calls "mature." Thus, he writes, the mature person will find himself at some points in his life at a place where the two ethics come together, as they must in anyone who has an identity of his or her own.

> I find it immeasurably moving when a *mature* [*reif*] human being—whether young or old in actual years is immaterial—who feels the responsibility he bears for the consequences of his own actions with his entire soul and who acts in harmony with an ethics of responsibility reaches the point where he says, "Here I stand, I can do no other." That is authentically human and cannot fail to move us [*ergreift*]. For this is a situation that *may* befall *any* of us at some point, if we are not inwardly dead. In this sense an ethics of conviction and an ethics of responsibility are not absolute antitheses but are mutually complementary, and only when taken together do they constitute the authentic human being [*echten Menschen*] who *is capable* of having a "vocation for politics." (P 92)

Weber claims here that a "mature" person, someone who lives in the world as an adult and not as a child, will at some point find himself at the intersection of his values and the facts of his life. To act / under these circumstances is to take both the conditions and terms of one's own life and values upon oneself and make them one's own. What does Weber mean here by the notion of maturity?[68] Only those who are "mature"—whose character manifests this quality—are entitled to claim the right to say honestly, "Here I stand, I can do

---

[68] While the emphasis on "maturity" goes back at least to Kant's *What is Enlightenment?* it becomes a central theme in nineteenth- and twentieth-century thought. The identification of maturity as a matter of central importance in Nietzsche, Weber, and Foucault has been made by David Owen, *Maturity and Modernity: Nietzsche, Weber, Foucault and the Ambivalence of Reason* (London and New York: Routledge, 1994). The link of Weber/Nietzsche and Foucault has been made previously. See Bryan S. Turner, "Nietzsche, Weber and the Devaluation of Politics: The Problem of State Legitimacy," *Sociological Review* 30 (1982): 367–91. See Mark Warren, "Max Weber's Liberalism for a Nietzschean World," *American Political Science Review* 82 (March 1988): 31–50.

no other." The reference to "old or young in years" calls forth the passage in the *Nicomachean Ethics*,[69] where Aristotle writes that a young man (whether young in years or in character) is not a fit subject for lectures in political science as he will tend to follow his passions and aim not at knowledge but at action. What kind of person is this? There are two preliminary elements to his conception of maturity.

First, for Weber, maturity is a kind of "trained ruthlessness" (*geschulte Rücksichtlosigkeit*)[70] in looking at the realities of the world, a refusal to avoid anything. It is an insistence that all possible targets, be they obscure social scientists or the top political leaders of Germany, be ruthlessly attacked. (The only exception that Weber will make to this is for friends, such as Robert Michels.) But just as neither "causality" nor "the materialist interpretation of history" are "hansom cabs to be picked up on an impulse,"[71] so also is the lot of the historical sociologist to deal with *all* aspects of the world that his science makes available to him.

This trained ruthlessness gives one the ability to face the realities of life and "bear and be adequate to them inwardly as an adult" (*sie zu ertragen und ihnen innerlich gewachsen zu sein*). Weber's metaphor is important and telling here. Anyone who cannot so do is still a "political infant." Indeed, "nine out of ten" of those whom Weber meets are such even when, perhaps especially when, they claim to be "mature." Weber here seeks in the notion of politics as a vocation to provide an exemplar to a disenchanted world of what a spiritually dignified public life would look like.[72] His metaphor is that of adulthood.[73]

It is at this point that Weber expands his discussion of those who cannot face the realities of the world as a grown-up, who lack maturity

---

[69] Aristotle, *Ethica Nicomachia* (Oxford: Clarendon, 1963), 1095a, 6–10.

[70] Gerth and Mills give this as "trained relentlessness," which has a very different flavor.

[71] P 89. Weber repeats the metaphor from P 81.

[72] See the interesting discussion in Hubert Treiber, "Nietzsche's Monastery for Free Spirits and Weber's Sect," in H. Lehmann and G. Roth, eds., *Weber's "Protestant Ethic": Origins, Evidence, Contexts* (Cambridge: Cambridge University Press, 1993), pp. 133–59. See also Harry Liebersohn, *Fate and Utopia in German Sociology, 1870–1923* (Cambridge, MA: MIT Press, 1988).

[73] This is a common metaphor in the period, found also in thinkers as diverse as Lenin and Freud. See David Owen, *Maturity and Modernity* (London and New York: Routledge, 1994), as well as Tracy Strong, "Psychoanalysis as a Vocation," *Political Theory* 12 (February 1984), 51–79.

and dignity. In the political realm they are the *Gesinnungspolitiker*, a word often translated as "politicians of conviction"[74] but which can also rendered as "politicians of predisposition" or "ideologists." *Gesinnung* in German means "convictions" or "fundamental belief." *Gesinnungslos* can mean "without principles." Weber here has in mind action that rests upon the conviction that one is right in some transcendental sense (*fiat justitia, pereat mundus* would be such an act).[75] These are those who interpret the world in such a manner so as to avoid facing the realities of their position in the world and especially the consequences that their actions will entail. Those who claim that they are going to eradicate the "false and the base," says Weber, are "spiritual lightweights" who have "become enraptured with romantic sensations."

For Weber, maturity—being an adult—is the recognition that any action taken is taken under circumstances where the consequences of that action are not only not apparent but over the long term do not add up to make sense (as Hegel had thought they would). The acceptance of this, and the avoidance of the plea of good intentions, no matter what the outcome, is what distinguishes an adult from a child. Mistakes are to be attributed to insufficient skill and commitment. Politics, as Hannah Arendt remarked in a similar vein, "is not the nursery." It does no good to say, "I didn't mean it."[76] Whether or not morality is the realm of deontology, politics is not, nor should it be thought to be so. One may think of such an outlook as tragic, meaning by tragedy the state of affairs that consists in the recognition that not only could one possibly do nothing to make the outcome of a state of affairs a happy one, but that one's very intention to set the world right itself led to disaster.

Lastly, responsible adulthood—and the making available of responsibility to others—requires Weber to distance his audience from their desires, much in the manner that the man who truly has the vocation for politics must have a distance on himself. This concern manifests itself especially in the way that Weber's text refuses to engage the hopes and expectations of his audience.

[74] Gerth and Mills, for instance, give it as "politics of conviction."

[75] "Let justice be done, and let the world perish." Weber writes (P 84): "With an ethics of conviction, one feels 'responsible' only for ensuring that the flame of pure conviction, for example, the flame of protest against the injustice of the social order, should never be extinguished."

[76] Hannah Arendt, *Eichmann in Jerusalem: A Report on the Banality of Evil* (New York: Viking, 1974), p. 279.

There is thus ultimately no division of facts and values when one's stance toward these matters places one's own being in the world on the line, such that one can authentically as one's own self "do no other." This moment—let us call it the "Lutheran moment"—is that time and space on which authentic individuality rests. What kind of moment is it? Weber is clearly not making a religious argument, nor is he making a moral one. The space and time in which one says "here I stand" is, however, one that legitimates the actions that are undertaken, legitimates them in the sense that one cannot but be impressed by those actions. (The moment is "authentically human and cannot fail to move us.")

In this context, one must ask oneself the significance of Weber's adducing Luther's claim to the entitlement of his being: "Here I stand, I can do no other." These are, famously, the words with which Luther concluded his defense before the Diet of Worms after he had been called upon to recant about half of his 95 Theses. It was, he said, wrong to go "against conscience," and it was on his own conscience that he, ineluctably, must find himself standing. Luther's announcement or confession marks and instantiates the moment in which he took his position in the world on himself. He proclaims that as he, to the best of his self-critical ability, finds himself in the world, so he is and will be for others. Only thus can his position have any integrity. For Weber such a moment is one that is taken in a kind of void. Nothing guarantees that this position will be the right one—it is nonetheless that for which one assumes responsibility. At Worms Luther went on to say that if anyone should take issue with his stance, that person should try to convince him of his error. Conscience, while absolute, is also importantly defeasible— and politics is not the nursery. The validity of a stance will be in the end (although only in the end) justifiable only in reference to the person who takes the responsibility for it upon himself.

3. The World as One Finds It

The self-knowledge to which Weber's text enjoins his audience as a prerequisite does not take them out of the world. Instead, it throws them back into it and places their feet on their own ground. Weber seeks neither escape from the world nor happiness in or after it.[77] But he does find in this world, as it is given to us as our history, the

---

[77] See the discussion below.

only possibility for humanness. In recognition of this, Weber is exceptionally conscious, here and throughout his work, that his understanding must take into account and speak from his own historical situation. That modern situation is one that he terms "*entzaubert*"—disenchanted or demagified. He attributes this to the progressive domination of rationalistic science, itself derived from salvation religion, that is, from Christianity. Crudely put, if one accepts that certain beliefs and or practices can ensure one's salvation, this implies that the world can be—difficult though it may be to do so in practice—controlled. The consequence of this rationalization has been specialization, such that each has only his task for his work with others. Thus the acceptance of the division of labor is the first step in the acceptance of the world in which one lives.

Yet for the world to be human—something Weber believes less and less—humans must face up to it ("like men," he writes). And facing up to the actualities of the demagified world in which we live requires that we be educated to it. Hence, the major concern in the "Politics" lecture is to set the preconditions for education to the world as it is and most especially to the political world. If the "Science" lecture responds to the question of "how is knowledge possible?" the "Politics" one is an answer to the question of "what (if anything) is to be done?"

The "Politics" lecture thus not only calls for political education but is itself a text *of* political education. Weber's concern for the political education of modern men and women, and of Germans in particular, preoccupied Weber throughout his career. Already in his *Inaugural Lecture* (1895), he had proclaimed: "For now we see one thing: an immense task of political education is to be accomplished, and no more serious task is set for us, each in his small circle, than to be conscious of this task: to contribute to the political education of our nation, something that must also be in particular the final goal of our science."[78]

Political education, as Weber conceives of it, consists in being trained to accept the realities of the world in which one lives. What would it mean to do so? A purpose of the "Politics" lecture is to set out what we might call terms of aesthetic entitlement. The problem

---

[78] From his *Inaugural Lecture* on GPS 30: "Für jetzt aber sehen wir eines: eine ungeheure politische Erziehungsarbeit ist zu leisten, und keine ernstere Pflicht besteht für uns, als, ein jeder in seinem kleinen Kreise, uns eben dieser Aufgabe bewußt zu sein: an der politischen Erziehung unserer Nation mitzuarbeiten, welche das letzte Ziel auch gerade unserer Wissenschaft bleiben muß."

is posed as follows. For Weber we live in a world that may be called polytheistic, a world in which "we find ourselves placed in different cultures [*Lebensordnungen*], each of which is subject to different laws" (P 87). What does this "polytheism" signify? As noted above, it might appear—as it did to several generations of Anglo-American social theorists—simply a statement of pluralism, familiar from the work of liberal political thought. One of the premises of liberalism, after all, is the recognition or claim that the values that the members of any society might seek to pursue are multiple and not necessarily of a piece. One might call this the historical actuality of pluralism.[79] For Weber, however, the matter is much more serious, not to say tragic. If we were to use Nietzsche's language we might phrase it as the reality of life after the death of God. Weber explains:

> The assumption that I am offering you here is based on a fundamental fact. This is that as long as life is left to itself and is understood in its own terms, it knows only that the conflict between these gods is never-ending. Or, in nonfigurative language, life is about the incompatibility of ultimate *possible* attitudes and hence the inability ever to resolve the conflicts between them. (S 27)

To interpret the world "in its own terms" is to live by an ethic of responsibility. If there is, in Alasdair MacIntyre's words, a "range of goods . . . accompanied by a recognition of a range of compartmentalized spheres within each of which some good is pursued: political, economic, familial, artistic, athletic, scientific,"[80] Weber's position is that the choice between these can never be made on the basis of commensurable values. The choice of one value slights another, and the only thing that can be done about it is to realize that this is what one is doing and to accept the responsibility for the consequences of the choice.

Weber's position has some affinity with that of Sir Isaiah Berlin, who writes in "Two Concepts of Liberty" that "the world we encounter in ordinary experience is one in which we are faced with choices between ends equally ultimate and claims equally absolute, the realization of some of which must inevitably involve the sacrifice

---

[79] For a discussion see Tracy B. Strong, "Setting One's Heart on Honesty: The Tensions of Liberalism and Religion," *Social Research* 66, 4 (Winter 1999), pp. 1143–66.

[80] Alasdair MacIntyre, *Whose Justice? Which Rationality?* (Notre Dame, IN: University of Notre Dame Press, 1988), p. 337.

of the other."[81] But Weber does not share Berlin's position that if human beings disagreed about ultimate matters then the political system that best allowed them to deal with the disagreements must privilege their liberty. Liberty carries no privilege for him.[82] Thus, while modern liberals derive from the fact of value pluralism the conclusion that the political realm should simply avoid consideration of ultimate questions, for Weber such avoidance is impossible.

His polytheism thus entails two nonliberal conclusions. First, it is a claim that there exists no transcendental realm, in morals or in politics, to which the justification of actions can be referred. Second, it is the claim that *each* of these value realms has an absolute claim on us. As long as one lives in the world, one cannot avoid them. While Weber will have admiration for those "virtuosos of unworldly goodness and the love for humankind" able to remove themselves from the world—he cites Platon Karatayev of Tolstoy's *War and Peace* and Father Zossima in Dostoyevsky's *The Brothers Karamazov* (P 90)—this is an admiration like that which Nietzsche's Zarathustra expresses as he comes down from the mountain for the old hermit who has not yet heard of the death of God: one can live that way but only in isolation from the world for which God's death is an ever increasing actuality. For the modern world there is no salvation of the soul, no matter how much those who hold to the ethics of conviction may want to believe that there may be.[83] The starting point for Weber is this separation. If one seeks "the salvation of one's soul" or indeed that of others, then one has not engaged in politics, "since politics faces quite different tasks, tasks that can only be accomplished with the use of force" (P 90).

With all this in mind we can now move to a question that might have seemed preliminary. What does Weber mean by politics? On the one hand, the matter is simple, for the "Politics" lecture gives a number of definitions. The term embraces "every kind of independent *leadership* activity" (P 32). As is constantly the case, Weber knows that the conditions of his lecture limit him to a narrower definition, here the leadership of a political association, which, in turn,

---

[81] Isaiah Berlin, *Four Essays on Liberty* (New York: Oxford University Press, 1969), p. 168.

[82] In the lecture (P 40), Weber refers to freedom simply as the lack of final princely authority.

[83] In this Weber harkens back to Machiavelli, who wrote to his friend Vettori that he "preferred the salvation of [his] city to that of [his] soul." See Niccolò Machiavelli, *The Chief Works and Others,* translated by Allan Gilbert (Durham, NC: Duke University Press, 1989), vol. 2, p. 1010.

he says means in the present day leadership in and/or of a state. Weber's famous definition of a state ("Nowadays, in contrast, we must say that the state is the form of human community that (successfully) lays claim to the *monopoly of legitimate physical violence* within a particular territory—and this idea of 'territory' is an essential defining feature" [P 33]) is thus importantly understood as that to which we are compelled "nowadays." Weber's point here is that whatever may have been meant by politics in other times and places (in Greece, for instance, or in the free cities of the Middle Ages),[84] today the *only* locus of politics is the state. The analysis of the vocation of politics—whether one lives "off" or "for" politics—takes place only within the context of the state.

Having claimed this, Weber proceeds on two fronts. First, he elaborates the realities and conditions of the world as the political personage encounters it. Second, he asks after the qualities of a person—the character of a personality—who is able to face these realities honestly and with personal and intellectual integrity.

The structure of "Politics as a Vocation," like that of the "Science" lecture, locates the source of human freedom, and indeed of humanity itself, inside a series of ever more constraining frameworks. The lecture begins with an elaboration of the universal qualities of politics, those that anyone engaging in political action will be required to acknowledge. It moves from there to a discussion of the evolution of politics in the West, the chain of developments that has given to the West its particular qualities. Subsequently, Weber analyzes the most developed forms of contemporary (Western) politics, particularly those in the United States, Great Britain, and Germany. By "most developed" Weber means those forms of political life that most clearly manifest the logic of historical development—one might say the "form"—of the modern world. These are now all states in which political leaders must get votes, just as modern *Wissenschaftler* must get students.

Only with this preliminary analysis of constraints in place is Weber then willing to turn to the conditions that individuals must face. As Peter Lassman has noted, for Weber it is "man's unavoidable fate to be a political animal,"[85] which today means that we

---

[84] See here Weber's analysis of the same in *Economy and Society,* part 2, chapter 8 (reprinted as *The City* [New York: Free Press, 1958]).

[85] Peter Lassman, "The Rule of Man over Man: Politics, Power and Legitimation," in Stephen Turner, ed., *The Cambridge Companion to Weber* (Cambridge: Cambridge University Press, 2000), p. 84.

must live in a state. It is, however, also the case that a characteristic of human behavior is to try to avoid one's fate. The tactic of starting with a description of the "steel casing" of externalities, as Weber calls them at the end of *The Protestant Ethic and the Spirit of Capitalism,* is precisely to enforce upon his audience the tragic nature of their situation. The externalities already eliminate many of the outcomes that most of his audience might want. Those to whom he speaks think they are in the springtime—at the time when all possibilities are open to them. Thus Weber will close the lecture with a mournful citation of Shakespeare's sonnet 102, about a time when "our love was new." Instead, now it is autumn and the wintry night of polar darkness is closing in upon them, although they do not acknowledge this as yet. There is, Weber writes, "tragedy in all action," but most deny it. Those who do not recognize this quality of the world are likely suddenly to collapse as products of "an exceedingly impoverished and superficial indifference toward the *meaning* of human activity, a blasé attitude that remains completely blind to the tragedy in which all action is ensnared, political action above all" (P 78).

4. WHAT ARE THE EXTERNAL REALITIES OF THE POLITICAL REALM?

The above discussion brought us back to the importance of the concrete actualities of the external conditions of the political. Politics, for Weber as for Aristotle, is about ruling and being ruled. In exploration of this we must thus examine what Weber means by *Herrschaft*.[86] In the lecture he defines the state in terms of its *Herrschaft*: "Like the political organizations that preceded it historically, the state represents a relationship in which people *rule over* other people.[87] This relationship is based on the legitimate use of force (that is to say, force that is perceived as legitimate)" (P 34). He proceeds to designate three types of legitimacy—the *traditional,* in which rule is legitimated by custom; the *charismatic,* in which the personal qualities of the ruler legitimate his actions; and the *"legal,"* in which rule rests upon the acceptance of "rationally constructed rules." The

---

[86] *Herrschaft* means "rule" or "power" or "authoritative power of command." It is translated most often as "authority" or "domination." One speaks in German of *Gott der Herr*—the Lord God.

[87] "Herrschaftsverhältnis von Menschen über Menschen."

external realities of the present-day political realm consist first and foremost in the ineluctability of the division of labor, and the consequent specialization of tasks defines the political realm, as in all other realms. If, however, there are three ideal types of domination or rule, it is clear that for Weber there can be no politics in the modern world that is not centrally involved with rational-legal *Herrschaft,* and this means with bureaucracy.

So the answer to the question of "What kind of historical beings are we?" is most simply that we are creatures who live under the conditions of general rationalization of social relationships, namely, the "bureaucratization of all forms of rule [*Herrschaft*]." By "bureaucratization of all forms of rule," Weber does not mean simply the system of organization by which large institutions govern their day-to-day affairs. In the "Politics" lecture, more than twenty pages—most of which was added by Weber in the printed version— are dedicated to an exploration of the nature of this form of rule. These pages recapitulate the analysis that he was making at length in *Economy and Society.*

In *Economy and Society* he argues that the general nature of *Herrschaft* designates "the situation in which the manifested will (command) of the ruler or rules is meant to influence the conduct of one or more others (the ruled) and actually does influence it in such a way that their conduct to a socially relevant degree occurs as if the ruled had made the content of the command the maxim of their conduct for its very own sake."[88]

There is more to this definition than might first appear. Weber apologizes for what he terms the "awkward" quality of the definition, pointing especially at the "'as if' formula." The "as if" in fact allows him to suggest that obedience occurs in a Kantian categorically imperative manner ("for its very own sake"), even though the command exists because someone has influenced the behavior of another. The reference to a "maxim of conduct" also draws attention to the Kantian resonances—the categorical imperative, Kant says, can be formulated as "Act according to a maxim which can be adopted at the same time as a universal law." Weber's formulation clearly draws on this but modifies it in accordance with his historical-sociological point of departure.

What is important here for our purposes is that in the modern rational-legal state, authoritatively engendered behavior is presently experienced *as if* it were autonomy. That is, it is the nature of the

---

[88] *Economy and Society* 946.

modern state that the ruled think that the rules under which they live are in fact rules for and by everyone, that is, their own rules. But what then is the autonomy experienced under the "bureaucratization of all forms of domination"? Bureaucracy, argues Weber, is a situation in which "obedience is . . . given to norms rather than to the person."[89] Bureaucracy is the form of human organization that rests on norms rather than persons, "laws" and not "men," as contemporary usage says approvingly. It is thus a form of domination in which commands are linked not to human beings but rather to abstract and nonpersonal entities. There is "'objective' discharge of business . . . according to calculable rules and 'without regard for persons.'"[90]

In this, bureaucracy is set by Weber in opposition to the political, for politics, Weber says, "means conflict," that is, a relation between *persons*. "Bureaucracy," Weber suggests, "failed completely whenever it was expected to deal with political problems." In fact, the two forms are "inherently alien" to each other.[91] In part this seems to be because bureaucracy effaces or disguises the fact that there is ruling going on at all—ruling being the defining quality of the political. Officials, even at the highest level, tend, says Weber, to think of themselves merely as the first official of their enterprise. Rules replace ruling, and "it is decisive for the modern loyalty to an office that in the pure type, it does not establish a relationship to a person, . . . but rather is devoted to impersonal and functional purposes."[92] Here Weber attaches himself again to Nietzsche and to the latter's anxieties about "all herd and no shepherd."[93] It is important to remember here that the lecture is about *politics* as a vocation—and thus sets itself in opposition to the dominant and necessary quality of the age, namely, the rationalization of roles of rule, that is, to bureaucracy.

This situation is all the more totalizing because it has abrogated to itself, Weber seems to indicate, much of the aura that used to

---

[89] Ibid., 954.

[90] Ibid., 975.

[91] "Parlament und Regierung im neugeordneten Deutschland" ("Parlament and Governance in a Reconstructed Germany"), GPS 170, *Economy and Society* 1417. Henceforth PG.

[92] *Economy and Society* 959.

[93] Compare this passage to Nietzsche, *The Gay Science,* para. 345: "our factory slaves . . . are used up . . . as part of a machine." See the discussion in Tracy B. Strong, *Friedrich Nietzsche and the Politics of Transfiguration* (Urbana: University of Illinois Press, 2000), chapter 7.

surround the old churches. Indeed, the process of depersonalization is not limited to politics. He writes:

> The political official—at least in the fully developed modern state— is not considered the personal servant of the ruler. Likewise, the bishop, the priest and the preacher are in fact no longer, as in early Christian times, carriers of a purely personal charisma, which offers other-worldly sacred values under the personal mandate of a master, and in principle only responsible to him, to everybody who appears worthy of them and asks for them. In spite of the partial survival of the old theory, they have become officials in the service of a func- tional purpose, a purpose which in the present-day "church" appears at once impersonal and ideologically sanctified.[94]

There are, however, human consequences for both individual and society when the procedures of bureaucratized domination supplant the choices of politics. Weber argues that to the degree that election (through some kind of voting, e.g., a plebiscite) plays no major role in the structuring of an organization, then that organization will tend to rationalize its procedures more easily, that is, to make them rule-governed. In fact, over the long term bureaucratic organization must devalue any power obtained through election, since that tends to lessen the claim to rational competence.

Weber writes:

> [T]he "separation" of the worker from the material means of pro- duction, destruction, administration, academic research [i.e., labor- ers, soldiers, civil servants, assistant professors] and finance in general is the common basis of the modern state, in its political, cul- tural and military spheres, and of private capitalist economy. In both cases, the disposition of these means is in the hands of that power whom the bureaucratic apparatus . . . directly obeys or to whom it is available in case of need. This apparatus is equally typical of all those organizations; its existence and function are inseparably cause and effect of this concentration of the means of operation. . . . Increasing public ownership (*Socialisierung*) in the economic sphere today unavoidably means increasing bureaucratization.[95]

A deadly process is initiated. Alienation encourages bureaucrati- zation, which encourages the sense of autonomy. This autonomy is, however, that of the "last men"—and Weber twice cites Nietzsche's

---

[94] *Economy and Society* 959.
[95] PG, GPS 141/*Economy and Society* 1394.

Thus Spoke Zarathustra specifically to this point.[96] To the degree that rational competence becomes a basis for social organization, the introduction of anything new to that framework (i.e., not legitimated in terms of that framework) will necessarily have to come from beyond that organization. In a bureaucracy the political problem is to find the sources of the new, sources that must come from outside the rationalized structure.[97] "The decisive question," Weber proclaims in "Parliament and Governance in a Reconstructed Germany," "about the future of Germany's political order must be: How can parliament be made fit to govern?"[98] As mentioned above, the reason this is now the central problem, he argues, is that "Bismarck had dishabituated [Germany] from worrying about public affairs, . . . [and] the nation [had] permitted itself to be talked into accepting something . . . which in truth amounted to the unchecked rule of the bureaucracy."[99] It is a matter of recruitment: since the "essence of politics is . . . struggle, the recruitment of allies and of a voluntary following," it is impossible to get training in this difficult art "under the career system of the *Obrigkeitsstaat* [the administrative state]."[100]

For Weber, over the long run, rationalization of social relationships runs counter to all forms of political democracy. At first, he allows, political democratization tends to increase and enhance social rationalization, for it encourages the notion that all individuals are to be treated on the same basis. But political decision-making procedures, he insists, are ultimately nonrational. The tendency to rationalization, therefore, will be to reduce the importance of procedures such as voting in face of more thoroughly rationalized and rule-governed processes. To the degree that this happens, specifically "human" solutions (ones that involve persons and thus rest on ultimately nonrational choices) will be increasingly devalued.

They will be attacked on the grounds that they are irrational, or nonrational, means to an end. The attack, however, will also be an attack on the idea that the means for social policies should be

---

[96] In *The Protestant Ethic and the Spirit of Capitalism* in *Religionssoziologie* 1, 204 (Parsons leaves out the reference in his translation: cf. p. 82).

[97] *Economy and Society* 961. See the discussion by Erik Olin Wright, "To Control or to Smash the Bureaucracy: Weber and Lenin on Politics, the State and Bureaucracy," *Berkeley Journal of Sociology* 19 (1974–5): 69–108, especially 70 f. Wright, however, focuses too much on a liberal-revolutionary dichotomy.

[98] PG, GPS 182/*Economy and Society* 1426.

[99] Ibid., GPS 166/*Economy and Society* 1413.

[100] Ibid., GPS 166/*Economy and Society* 1414.

human means. Rules that make, or appear to make, a claim to universality in effect deny the historical and human quality of decisions and policies. Weber writes: "It is decisive for the specific nature of modern loyalty to an office, that, in the pure type, it does not establish a relation to a person, like a vassal's or disciple's faith in feudal or patrimonial relations of authority. Modern loyalty is devoted to an impersonal functional [*sachlichen*] purpose [*Zweck*]."[101] For Weber there is a real danger that persons and thus the nonrational will be eliminated from the modern world.

One should note at this point, however, that Weber is caught in a paradox. The historical nature of human beings in the present is to be increasingly without an historical nature. Before exploring his approach to this paradox, a number of additional factors that complicate the world even more must be examined.

In relation to the conduct of political and social life, the entire quality of human relations is affected by the rationalization of society. Weber notes that rationalization tends to promote situations where business is discharged according to calculable rules and without regard for "persons." Furthermore, the notion of legitimacy that corresponds to this pattern of authority tends to reinforce it in the minds of those subject to it. We think, for instance, that there is something wrong or unjust if an individual waiting to pay his or her bill at the cashier's is either given special treatment or denied equal treatment because of race, sex, religion, or social origin. In this case, the person would have been treated in terms of his or her particular characteristics, that is, not in terms of universal categories. Even one hundred years ago in the West, this would not have been so widely the case. What we want is for everyone to be treated the same— there are attractive things about bureaucracy and the rationalized pattern of authority.

These processes extend themselves into other realms. The discharge of business without regard for persons—*sine ira et studio*— is, in the words of Weber, "also the watchword of the market place and, in general, of all pursuits of naked economic interests." Hence the bureaucratization of society means, in fact, the domination of those classes (defined in purely economic terms here) that will profit from the market, that is, of the rich. Weber continues explicitly: "If the principle of the free market is not at the same time restricted, [this] means the universal domination of the 'class situation.'"[102]

---

[101] *Economy and Society* 959.

[102] Ibid., 975.

The antipolitical qualities of bureaucracy—politics again being for Weber a relation between persons and not between law-defined roles—tend thus to encourage the domination of the market over politics or, more precisely, over what is left of politics.

A Marxist analysis might have said that the domination of the market over politics encourages bureaucratization. Weber and Marx see the same things, but as they arrive at their diagnoses from very different paths, their conclusions are correspondingly different. In particular, Weber does not understand class consciousness as resulting from the obvious domination of politics by economics. Rather, he argues, no common consciousness is formed. By eliminating persons and replacing them with roles, there is no need for a common consciousness. "Bureaucracy develops the more perfectly, the more it is 'dehumanized,' the more completely it succeeds in eliminating from official business love, hatred, and all purely personal, irrational, and emotional elements which escape calculation. This is appraised as its special virtue by capitalism."[103]

Bureaucracy is thus the front of a great historical process of rationalization that has as its consequence the increasing destruction of affective or status relations between individuals and the progressive domination of the economic over the political.[104] The bureaucrat is in fact the vanguard of history, implicitly a participant in a vast revolutionary process that has totally transformed all relationships. Weber sketches this out in the last pages of the "Bureaucracy" section of *Economy and Society*. The democratic ethos is tied in with specific substantive questions (on rights, for example) that are not a necessary part of a rational-legal system;[105] the rational-legal system is only instrumentally oriented. Such instrumentality can make use of "rights" and so forth, but rights are clearly only instruments to its instrumentality. In fact, Weber claims, instrumentality has become the world historical *Zweck* for the West. Where there arises a conflict between the substantive parts of the democratic ethos—treating an individual not only fairly, but with dignity, for example—there also arises an incompatibility between bureaucratic procedures and democracy. This incompatibility will most especially be of importance to those in the lower classes, since by what we noted above,

---

[103] Ibid.

[104] See here Karl Löwith, "Marx und Weber," in *Gesammelte Abhandlungen: Zur Kritik der geschichtlichen Existenz* (Stuttgart: Kohlhammer Verlag, 1960), pp. 1–3.

[105] See here Max Weber, *The Religion of China: Confucianism and Taoism* (New York: Free Press, 1968), pp. 226–49.

they will be increasingly subject to those who have money, to those classes, that is, who will naturally come to dominate the bureaucracy.

This is a little known part of Weber where, although in no ways "Marxist," he deals with the same constellation of circumstances as does Marx. He writes: "The propertyless masses especially are not served by the formal 'equality before the law' and the 'calculable' adjudication and administration demanded by bourgeois interests."[106] Thus for Weber, under the bureaucracy those who suffer from the historical process the most are the working classes.

His position here is far more complex than most standard arguments about the "rise of mass society." It is a mistake to see Weber's position as noting with a sad, grey regret the decline of the aristocracy and the rise of the plebs and faceless anonymity. He is rather reasserting an argument that he had made elsewhere against Gustav Schmoller, Wilhelm Roscher, and others,[107] to the effect that although it is in the *nature* of the bureaucracy to be "neutral" and instrumental, it is not and cannot be the *practice* of the bureaucracy to so remain. In fact, Weber argues that the practice of bureaucratic domination goes "hand in hand with the concentration of the material means of management in the hand of the master,"[108] and that this process occurs in both business and public organizations.

This is the central development of modern society. As Robert Eden has pointed out,[109] to live by the division of labor as a member of the bureaucracy is to partake of the most widespread revolutionary process in the world. Marx had argued in the *Communist Manifesto* that it was in the nature and to the glory of the bourgeoisie that it wipe out all structures that threatened to become permanent. "All that is solid melts into thin air," he wrote, signifying that the Faustian urge of the bourgeoisie would tolerate nothing to remain in the form it was, neither human relations nor commodities.[110] Weber's vision is a cousin to Marx's but with real family differences. It is also true for him that bourgeois society, as expressed socially in

---

[106] *Economy and Society* 980; see also 990 ff.

[107] See Manfred Schön, "Gustav Schmoller and Max Weber," in Wolfgang J. Mommsen and Jürgen Osterhammel, eds., *Max Weber and His Contemporaries* (London: German Historical Institute, 1987); and Guy Oakes, introduction to *Roscher and Knies,* p. 19.

[108] *Economy and Society* 980.

[109] Eden, *Political Leadership and Nihilism.*

[110] See the discussion of this passage from the *Manifesto* in Marshall Berman, *All That Is Solid Melts into Thin Air: The Experience of Modernity* (New York: Simon and Schuster, 1982), chapter 1.

rationalized structures, tends to eliminate anything that is solid. But the "solids" that melt—love, friendship, passion, hatred, marriage, honor, and so forth—are specifically human relations, not just those of the stages prior to the full realization of the bourgeoisie. For Weber the bureaucracy leaves nothing as it was and transforms previous orders into its own rational vision. To be a bureaucrat is not only not to be a person but also to participate in a historical transformation of the world, far more extensive than any that particular political groups or parties could advocate. Bureaucrats are the locomotive of the train of historical rationalism, destroying all other structures of domination.[111]

Rationalization and bureaucratization are ensured both an objective and a subjective basis of perpetuation. As Weber remarks at the end of *The Protestant Ethic and the Spirit of Capitalism*:

> The Puritan wanted to be a person of calling—we must be one. For when asceticism was carried out of monastic cells into the life of calling and began to dominate ordinary morality, it did its part in building the tremendous cosmos of the modern economic order, bound as it is to the technical and economic preconditions of the mechanically based production that today predestines with overpowering compulsion the life patterns of all those born into this engine—not just those directly concerned with economic activity—and perhaps will so predestine them until the last hundred weight of fossilized fuel is burnt. In Baxter's view the care for external goods should only lie on the shoulders of its saints "like a light cloak that can be thrown aside at any moment." But fate decreed that the cloak should become a steel casing. As asceticism undertook to remake the world and to work itself out in the world, external goods have acquired an increasing and in the end inexorable power over humans, such as never before seen in history. Today its spirit—whether finally, who knows?—has escaped from its casing.[112]

---

[111] *Economy and Society* 1002.

[112] *Gesammelte Aufsätze zur Max Weber Religionssoziologie* (Tübingen: Mohr, 1947), vol. 1, pp. 203–4: Der Puritaner wollte Berufsmensch sein,—wir müssen es sein. Denn indem die Askese aus den Mönchszellen heraus in das Berufsleben übertragen wurde und die innerweltliche Sittlichkeit zu beherrschen begann, half sie an ihrem Teile mit daran, jenen mächtigen Kosmos der modernen, an die technischen und ökonomischen Voraussetzungen mechanisch-maschineller Produktion gebundenen, Wirtschaftsordnung erbauen, der heute den Lebensstil aller einzelnen, die in dies Triebwerk hineingeboren werden—nicht nur der direkt ökonomisch Erwerbstätigen—, mit überwältigendem Zwange bestimmt und vielleicht bestimmen wird, bis der letzte Zentner fossilen Brennstoffs verglüht ist. Nur wie "ein dünner Mantel, den man jederzeit abwerfen könnte," sollte nach Baxters Ansicht die Sorge um die

In such conditions, ruling is impossible without a bureaucracy.[113] Furthermore, Weber tells us, since bureaucracy bears no necessary relation to any given political economic system, the drive toward perpetuation will take place under both Socialist and capitalist states.[114]

Weber implies, indeed *asserts,* that under no foreseeable conditions will life in other than a rationalized society henceforth be possible. Here his attitude toward the division of labor is importantly different from that of his other two great social scientist contemporaries, Marx and Emile Durkheim. The dream of doing away with the division of labor that had attracted Marx as well as the Utopian Socialists seems to Weber a pointless dream. There was no hope for what Lenin was at about the same period to anticipate hopefully, the slow reemergence of "the elementary rules of social life that have been known for centuries."[115] In the famous image cited above from the end of *The Protestant Ethic and the Spirit of Capitalism,* we live rather in an "iron cage," or, in a more accurate translation, in a "steel casing" (*stahlhartes Gehäuse*), outside of which there is nothing we can see.

Nor does Weber think, as did Durkheim, that the social division of labor is necessary because society and justice are founded upon it.[116] Rather, Weber thinks, as does Marx, that the historical process and not the functional basis of society is the most important thing to look at in understanding the human world. Weber thinks that rationalization—a form of theodicy—is the force that animates history and that no one has a choice, if they are honest with themselves, but to acknowledge themselves as a subject of that force. Thus, what Marx had seen as the source of human alienation—the socially

---

äußeren Güter um die Schultern seiner Heiligen liegen. Aber aus dem Mantel ließ das Verhängnis ein stahlhartes Gehäuse werden. Indem die Askese die Welt umzubauen und in der Welt sich auszuwirken unternahm, gewannen die äußeren Güter dieser Welt zunehmende und schließlich unentrinnbare Macht über den Menschen, wie niemals zuvor in der Geschichte. Heute ist ihr Geist—ob endgültig, wer weiß es?—aus diesem Gehäuse entwichen. The passage is poorly translated in PESC 181.

[113] *Economy and Society* 990; cf. Mommsen, *Max Weber und die deutsche Politik* (Tübingen: Mohr, 1959), pp. 97, 121.

[114] *Economy and Society* 988.

[115] V. I. Lenin, "State and Revolution," in *Selected Works,* vol. 1, part 1 (Moscow: Foreign Languages Publishing House, 1950), p. 74.

[116] See the letters from Marcel Mauss cited in Raymond Aron, *Memoires: 50 ans de reflexions* (Paris: Juillard, 1983), p. 71.

forced and necessary division of labor—is in fact for Weber the fundamental precondition and characteristic of human life in the modern world.[117] It is still "alienation" for Weber but with the difference that there is in fact nothing else to be alienated from. Thus we can no more live without the division of labor implied by bureaucracy than we can get off the track of history.[118]

There is no way around this problem. The inevitability of bureaucracy has nothing to do with its power or potential power. Indeed, Weber wrote to his friend and student Michels in November 1906 that "indispensability in the economic process means nothing, absolutely nothing in the power position and power chances of the class."[119] The importance of the bureaucracy derives solely from the fact that it comes to structure alterations in its own image, and the ruler, Weber says, is helpless unless "he finds support in Parliament," that is, from an outside and nonrational source.

5. WHO MIGHT ACT POLITICALLY: CHARISMA AND MEANING FOR LIFE

We have been examining the historical characteristics of the world that govern the significance we can attribute to cultural phenomena. How then do beings such as those described above—ourselves—understand the world while fully acknowledging their position in it? If the world is for Weber, as noted above, inexhaustible chaos, then the source and validity of the understanding of this world must be derived not from "facts" about the world but from the quality of character of a person of knowledge. What kind of person must one be—what must one have acknowledged about one's historicity—in order to be able to make, to be entitled to make, "objective" claims about our condition?

---

[117] Compare the argument about Marx and Durkheim in Steven Lukes, "Alienation and Anomie," in P. Laslett and W. Runciman, eds., *Politics, Philosophy and Society,* series I and II (Oxford: Blackwell, 1967), pp. 134–55.

[118] GPS 321–2/*Economy and Society* 1394. We thus agree with Lawrence Scaff, "Max Weber and Robert Michels," *American Journal of Sociology* 86, no. 6 (1981): 1269–86, and with Fredric Jameson, "The Vanishing Mediator: Narrative Structure in Max Weber," *New German Critique* 1 (Winter 1973): 52–89, as well as with Bryan Turner, *For Weber* (London and Boston: Routledge and Kegan Paul, 1981), that there is a "structuralism" in Weber, although we see it as much more diachronic than do they.

[119] Cited from Wolfgang Mommsen, *Max Weber und die deutsche Politik,* p. 97; see Scaff, "Max Weber and Robert Michels," 1281–3.

Weber's hope for such individuals is at the core of his valuation of the other main category of modern legitimacy, namely, rule by the "charismatic leader." At the beginning of the "Politics" lecture he indicates that he will be most concerned with the charismatic ruler, despite the fact that he describes the modern situation as disenchanted and rationalized in the manner we have just examined. It is only in the charismatic leader that Weber finds the possibility for overcoming the dehumanizing regularization of the rationalized world. Thus, speaking of the price one pays for having leadership, he writes, "But there is only this stark choice: either a democracy with a leader together with a 'machine' or a leaderless democracy, in other words, the rule of the 'professional politicians' who have no vocation and who lack the inner, charismatic qualities that turn a man into a leader" (P 75).

In Weber's vision the only possibility of "reenchanting" a world grown grey with rationalization is for a leader possessed by and possessing a "gift of grace" such that his very person legitimizes his rule. Much has been written in criticism of Weber on this count, the most extreme version being that of Wolfgang Mommsen, who accused Weber of laying the groundwork for fascism.[120] This is a complex question, raising matters that cannot be dealt with here. Weber certainly holds out hope for the charismatic plebiscitarian leader, but he also, we think, establishes such stringent criteria that such a leader must meet as to make the actual existence of a real leader close to impossible. What is often ignored here is that, on this score, his mode immediately becomes Augustinian. In 410 Augustine had with great circumspection come to the conclusion over the course of his conflict with Bishop Donatus' (soon to be) heretic followers that under certain conditions coercion should and could be used in the name of Christian love. The salvation of souls was of an importance so paramount that humans could be coerced against their immediate (and misunderstanding) wills to accept baptism. This raised immediately the question of who should do the coercing, that is, of the qualities that a prince must have. Augustine argued that only those who were acting from true love could be entitled to use such coercion.[121]

---

[120] Mommsen, *Max Weber und die deutsche Politik*. See also his partial retractions after criticism in *The Age of Bureaucracy* (Oxford: Blackwell, 1974).

[121] Augustine, letter 185, in *Letters*, vol. 3 (New York: Catholic Publishers, 1953). See the discussion in Peter Brown, *Augustine of Hippo* (Berkeley and Los Angeles: University of California Press, 1975), especially pp. 233–43.

In a similar manner, in "Politics as a Vocation" Weber's discussion of the personal characteristics that the political leader must have in order to be entitled to act so as to weld people together into a community is designed to keep people from following false prophets and, not incidentally, to prevent too easy claims to such prophecy. Under what conditions does the political leader exist? The answer is that he exists under the same conditions as everyone else, subject to the disenchantment of the world, the polytheism of values, the necessity for specialization, and the division of labor—except that he has the ability to "bear" it. The point of the lecture is both to make clear the importance and the attraction of political leadership in the contemporary disenchanted world and to keep citizens from succumbing too easily to their desire for answers. The structure of the lecture, as we have expounded it, exemplifies the critical self-clarity for which it calls.

In "Politics as a Vocation" Weber spends much time describing both the bureaucratization of the world and the necessity of accepting it while concomitantly insisting on the reality that we are "placed into different cultures (*Lebensordnungen*), each of which is subject to different laws" (P 87). The premises of the political sphere are thus approximately those of the scientific one. Any action, including a political action, will constitute an attribution of meaning. We know that all general claims to meaning are invalid; yet the world is filled with those who have not the self-discipline to hold unto themselves the world in all its chaos. We must make something of the world and not take our action as other than it is. "Seeing how much I can bear" is the premise of facing both the scientific and political worlds as they are.

David Owen

Tracy B. Strong

A Note on the Translation

These lectures have been translated twice before. Both lectures appear in Hans Gerth and C.W. Mills, eds., *From Max Weber* (New York: Oxford University Press, 1961 and later editions). The "Politics" lecture appears in P. Lassman and R. Speirs, *Weber: Political Writings* (Cambridge: Cambridge University Press, 1994) and the "Science" lecture in P. Lassman and I. Velody, eds., *Max Weber's "Science as a Vocation"* (London: Unwin Hyman, 1989).

It is a hermeneutical commonplace to remark that all translations are a form of interpretation, a response to what the translators see as the matter of the text. The Gerth and Mills translations respond to the perceived need of the translators to establish a general scientific and critical sociology for the English-speaking world. They thereby pass over the philosophical attentions of Weber's language: the Weber who emerges is a sociologist with apparently little concern for philosophical matters and questions. The two other translations aim at producing a more contemporary, broad, scholarly voice but are less attentive to the rhetorical strategies of Weber's language. The ones in this volume by the well-known scholar and translator Rodney Livingstone attempt to remedy both of these deficiencies without sacrificing any of the rigors and strengths of the other translations. We have also provided the German text for particularly important passages from Weber's other works.

Interpretation is one thing; voice is another. For instance, a comparison of the last few pages of Talcott Parsons' translation of *The Protestant Ethic and the Spirit of Capitalism* with the German text shows that Parsons was simply deaf to the Nietzschean references and resonances (e.g., to "last men") in Weber and simply glossed over them. We have tried here to preserve these resonances.

The footnotes to the lectures are mostly the product of the learning and work of Rodney Livingstone. The editors thank him deeply for this and his many other contributions to this project.

TEXTS OF WEBER IN GERMAN

A new scholarly edition of Weber is under way. All of his work, published and not, will eventually appear in the *Gesamtausgabe* (of which sixteen volumes as well as four volumes of the letters had appeared as of the end of 2003).

Max Weber, *Gesamtausgabe.* On behalf of the Kommission fuer Sozial- und Wirtschaftsgeschichte der Bayerischen Akademie der Wissenschaften. Edited by Horst Baier, M. Rainer Lepsius, Wolfgang J. Mommsen, Wolfgang Schluchter, and Johannes Winckelmann. Tübingen: Mohr, Continuing edition.

Some of this material will also appear in a paperback *Studienausgabe,* without most of the research apparatus (ten volumes as of the end of 2003). The volume of the *Studienausgabe* that includes the two lectures translated in this volume is:

Max Weber, *Wissenschaft als Beruf (1917/1919) Politik als Beruf (1919).* Edited by Wolfgang J. Mommsen and Wolfgang Schluchter with the collaboration of Birgitt Morgenbrod. Tübingen: Mohr, 1994.

The older edition of Weber from Mohr lacks philological and scholarly editing and includes the following volumes:

Max Weber, *Gesammelte Politische Schriften* (Tübingen: Mohr, 1958)—includes "Politics as a Vocation."

Max Weber, *Gesammelte Aufsätze zur Wissenschaftslehre* (Tübingen: Mohr, 1968)—includes "Science as a Vocation."

Weber gave both lectures from notes, what the Germans call *Stichwörter* (keywords or cues). The lectures were written down stenographically. The "Science" lecture was published much as it was delivered, but its *Stichwörter* evidently have not survived. Weber added some material to the "Politics" lecture before publication. A facsimile of *Stichwörter* for that lecture, filled with Weber's apparently last-minute intercalations, has survived. In both of the new German editions it is reproduced after the text of the lecture and gives a strong impression of the notes Weber had in front of him. The interested reader may consult the new German editions listed here.

Major Texts of Weber in English

Weber: Political Writings. Edited by Peter Lassman and Ronald Speirs. Cambridge: Cambridge University Press, 1994. A generally excellent edition of the writings concerned with politics, many of them newspaper articles.

Max Weber's "Science as a Vocation." Edited by Peter Lassman and Irving Velody. London: Unwin Hyman, 1989.

From Max Weber. Edited by Hans Gerth and C. Wright Mills. New York: Oxford University Press, 1961. The still classic edition of Weber's work in English with a good selection (including the two lectures) oriented toward sociology rather than the other elements of Weber's work.

Economy and Society. Berkeley and Los Angeles: University of California Press, 1978. A compendium of other translations, some good, others less so. Includes "Parliament and Governance in a Reconstructed Germany" as an appendix.

The Protestant Ethic and the Spirit of Capitalism. Edited and translated by Talcott Parsons. New York: Scribner's, 1958. An often unreliable translation and edition but still in print. Two new translations have appeared: (1) *The Protestant Ethic and the Spirit of Capitalism.* New introduction and translation by Stephen Kalhberg. Chicago and London: Fitzroy Dearborn, 2001. (2) *The Protestant Ethnic and the "Spirit" of Capitalism and Other Writings.* Edited and translated with an introduction by Peter Baehr and Gordon C. Wells. New York: Penguin Books, 2002.

The Methodology of the Social Sciences. Translated and edited by Edward A. Shils and Henry A. Finch. New York: Free Press, 1949. Contains Weber's most important writings on methodology.

The Essential Weber: A Reader. Edited by Sam Whimster. London: Routledge, 2003.

The Protestant Ethic Debate: Max Weber's Replies to His Critics, 1907–10. Translated by Mary Shields. Edited by David Chalcraft and Austin Harrington. Manchester: Manchester University Press, 2001. Contains four important replies by Weber to reviews of PESC by two German historians of the day, H. Karl Fischer and Felix Rachfahl.

FURTHER READING

The following list of readings supplements those found in the footnotes to this introduction. An excellent selection of articles on Weber can be found in:

Hamilton, Peter, ed. *Max Weber: Critical Assessments.* 4 vols. London: Routledge, 1992.

Beyond these, there is an enormous amount of material in many languages. Good English-language sources include:

Albrow, Martin. *Max Weber's Construction of Social Theory.* New York: St. Martin's Press, 1990.

Andreski, Stanislav. *Max Weber's Insights and Errors.* London: Routledge and Kegan Paul, 1985.

Aron, Raymond. *German Sociology.* Glencoe, IL: Free Press, 1957.

Arrighi, Giovanni, and Terence K. Hopkins. "Theoretical Space and Space for Theory in World-Historical Social Science." In Norbert Wiley, ed., *The Marx-Weber Debate,* pp. 31–41. Newbury Park, CA: Sage, 1987.

Axtmann, Roland. "The Formation of the Modern State: A Reconstruction of Max Weber's Arguments." *History of Political Thought* 11 (Summer 1990): 295–311.

Beetham, David. "Max Weber and the Liberal Political Tradition." In Asher Horowitz and Terry Maley, eds., *The Barbarism of Reason,* pp. 99–112. Toronto: University of Toronto Press, 1994.

———. *Max Weber and the Theory of Modern Politics.* London: Allen and Unwin, 1974; Cambridge: Polity Press, 1995.

Bellamy, Richard. "Liberalism and Nationalism in the Thought of Max Weber." *History of European Ideas* 14, no. 4 (July 1992): 499–507.

Bendix, Reinhard. *Max Weber: An Intellectual Portrait.* Garden City, NY: Doubleday, 1960.

Bendix, Reinhard, and Günther Roth. *Scholarship and Partisanship: Essays on Max Weber.* Berkeley: University of California Press, 1971.

Benhabib, Seyla. "Rationality and Social Action: Critical Reflection on Weber's Methodological Writings." *Philosophical Forum* 12 (Summer 1981): 356–74.

Blum, Fred H. "Max Weber: The Man of Politics and the Man Dedicated to Objectivity and Rationality." *Ethics* 70 (October 1959): 1–20.

Blustone, Leslie D. *Max Weber's Theory of the Family.* Millwood, NY: Associated Faculty Press, 1987.

Boudon, Raymond. "Weber and Durkheim: Beyond the Differences, a Common Important Paradigm?" *Revue International de Philosophie* 2, no. 192 (1995): 221–39.

Breiner, Peter. *Max Weber and Democratic Politics.* Ithaca, NY: Cornell University Press, 1996.

———. "The Political Logic of Economics and the Economic Logic of Modernity in Max Weber." *Political Theory* 23 (1995): 25–48.

Brugger, Winfried. "Max Weber and Human Rights as the Ethos of the Modern Era." *Philosophy and Social Criticism* 9 (Fall/Winter 1982): 257–80.

Bruun, H. H. *Science, Values and Politics in Max Weber's Methodology.* Copenhagen: Munksgaard, 1972.

Burger, Thomas. *Max Weber's Theory of Concept Formation, Historical Laws, and Ideal Types.* Durham, NC: Duke University Press, 1976.

Burris, Val. "The Neo-Marxist Synthesis of Marx and Weber on Class." In Norbert Wiley, ed., *The Marx-Weber Debate,* pp. 67–90. Newbury Park, CA: Sage, 1987.

Chowers, Eyal. "Disciplining the Personality: Self and Social Critique in Max Weber's Work." *History of Political Thought* 15, no. 3 (Autumn 1994): 447–60.

Clague, Monique. "Conceptions of Leadership, Charles De Gaulle and Max Weber." *Political Theory* 3 (November 1975): 423–40.

Cohen, Jean. "Max Weber and the Dynamics of Rationalized Domination." *Telos* 14 (Winter 1972): 63–86.

Collins, Randall. *Weberian Sociological Theory*. Cambridge: Cambridge University Press, 1986.

———. "Weber's Last Theory of Capitalism: A Systematization." In Mark Granovetter and Richard Swedberg, eds., *The Sociology of Economic Life,* pp. 95–113. Boulder, CO: Westview Press, 1992.

Dallmayr, Fred. "Max Weber and the Modern State." In Asher Horowitz and Terry Maley, eds., *The Barbarism of Reason,* pp. 44–63. Toronto: University of Toronto Press, 1994.

Dickson, T., and H. V. McLachlan. "In Search of the 'Spirit of Capitalism': Weber's Misinterpretation of Franklin." *Sociology* 23 (1989): 81–9.

Diggins, John Patrick. *Max Weber: Politics and the Spirit of Tragedy*. New York: Basic Books, 1996.

Dronberger, Ilse. *The Political Thought of Max Weber: Quest of Statesmanship*. New York: Appleton-Century-Crofts, 1971.

Eden, Robert. "Doing without Liberalism: Weber's Regime Politics." *Political Theory* 10 (August 1982): 379–408.

———. *Political Leadership and Nihilism: A Study of Weber and Nietzsche*. Gainesville: University Press of Florida, 1983.

Edgar, Andrew. "Weber, Nietzsche, and Music." In Peter R. Sedgwick, *Nietzsche: A Critical Reader,* pp. 84–103. Cambridge: Blackwell, 1995.

Eisenstadt, Shmuel N., ed. *The Protestant Ethic and Modernization: A Comparative View*. New York: Basic Books, 1968.

Ewing, Sally. "Formal Justice and the Spirit of Capitalism: Max Weber's Sociology of Law." *Law and Society Review* 3 (1987): 487–512.

Ferrarotti, Franco. *Max Weber and the Crisis of Western Civilization*. Millwood, NY: Associated Faculty Press, 1987.

———. *Max Weber and the Destiny of Reason*. Translated by John Fraser. Armonk, NY: M. E. Sharpe, 1982.

Freund, Julien. *Max Weber*. Paris: Presses Universitaires de France, 1969.

Giddens, Anthony. *Capitalism and Modern Social Theory: An Analysis of the Writings of Marx, Durkheim and Max Weber*. London: Cambridge University Press, 1971.

Goddard, David. "Max Weber and the Objectivity of Social Science." *History and Theory* 12 (1973): 1–22.

Goldman, Harvey. *Max Weber and Thomas Mann: Calling and Shaping of the Self*. Berkeley and Los Angeles: University of California Press, 1988.

———. *Politics, Death, and the Devil: Self and Power in Max Weber and Thomas Mann*. Berkeley and Los Angeles: University of California Press, 1992.

Hardtwig, Wolfgang. "Jacob Burckhardt and Max Weber: Two Concepts of the Origin of the Modern World." In Reginald Lilly, ed., *The Ancients and the Moderns*, pp. 170–83. Bloomington: Indiana University Press, 1996.

Heins, Volker. "Weber's Ethic and the Spirit of Anti-capitalism." *Political Theory* 41 (1993): 269–84.

Hekman, Susan. "Max Weber and Post-positivist Social Theory." In Asher Horowitz and Terry Maley, eds., *The Barbarism of Reason*, pp. 267–86. Toronto: University of Toronto Press, 1994.

———. *Weber, The Ideal Type, and Contemporary Social Theory*. Notre Dame, IN: University of Notre Dame Press, 1983.

Honigsheim, Paul. "Max Weber, His Religious and Ethical Background and Development." *Church History* 19 (1950): 219–39.

———. *On Max Weber*. New York: Free Press, 1968.

Honnefelder, Ludger. "Rationalization and Natural Law: Max Weber's and Ernst Troeltsch's Interpretation of the Medieval Doctrine of Natural Law." *Review of Metaphysics* 49, no. 2 (December 1995): 275–94.

Horowitz, Asher. "The Comedy of Enlightenment, Weber, Habermas, and the Critique of Reification." In Asher Horowitz and Terry Maley, eds., *The Barbarism of Reason*, pp. 195–222. Toronto: University of Toronto Press, 1994.

Horowitz, Irving Louis. "The Protestant Weber and the Spirit of American Sociology." *History of European Ideas* 3 (1982): 415–28.

Huff, Toby E. *Max Weber and the Methodology of the Social Sciences*. New Brunswick, NJ: Transaction Books, 1984.

Jaspers, Karl. *On Max Weber*. New York: Paragon House, 1989.

Kee, Howard Clark. "Weber Revisited." In Leroy Rouner, ed., *Meaning, Truth, and God*. Notre Dame, IN: University of Notre Dame Press, 1982.

Kolko, Gabriel. "A Critique of Max Weber's Philosophy of History." *Ethics* 70 (October 1959): 21–36.

————. "Max Weber on America: Theory and Evidence." *History and Theory* 1 (1961): 243–60.

Krygier, Martin. "Weber, Lenin, and the Reality of Socialism." In Eugene Kamenka and Martin Krygier, eds., *Bureaucracy: The Career of a Concept,* pp. 61–87. New York: St. Martin's Press, 1979.

Lachmann, Ludwig Maurits. *The Legacy of Max Weber: Three Essays.* London: Heinemann, 1970.

Landmann, Michael. "Critiques of Reason from Weber to Bloch." *Telos* 29 (Fall 1976): 187–98.

Lash, Scott, and Sam Whimster, eds. *Max Weber, Rationality and Modernity.* London: Allen and Unwin, 1987.

Lehmann, Hartmut, and Günther Roth, eds. *Weber's "Protestant Ethic": Origins, Evidence, Contexts.* Cambridge: Cambridge University Press, 1993.

Lempert, Richard. "The Force of Irony: On the Morality of Affirmative Action and 'United Steelworkers' versus 'Weber,' *Ethics* 95 (October 1984): 86–9.

Lenhardt, Christian. "Max Weber and the Legacy of Critical Idealism." In Asher Horowitz and Terry Maley, eds. *The Barbarism of Reason,* pp. 21–48. Toronto: University of Toronto Press, 1994.

Little, David. *Religion, Order, and Law: A Study in Pre-revolutionary England.* Chicago: University of Chicago Press, 1984.

Love, John. "Max Weber and the Theory of Ancient Capitalism." *History and Theory* 25 (May 1986): 152–72.

Lowenstein, Karl. *Max Weber's Political Ideas in the Perspective of Our Time.* Amherst, MA: University of Massachusetts Press, 1966.

Löwith, Karl. *Max Weber and Karl Marx.* London: George, Allen and Unwin, 1982.

Lowy, Michael. "Weber Against Marx?" *Science and Society* 53 (1989): 71–84.

Maley, Terry. "The Politics of Time, Subjectivity and Modernity in Max Weber." In Asher Horowitz and Terry Maley, eds., *The Barbarism of Reason,* pp. 139–68. Toronto: University of Toronto Press, 1994.

McIntosh, Donald. "Husserl, Weber, Freud, and the Method of the Human Sciences." *Philosophy of the Social Sciences* 27, no. 3 (September 1997): 328–53.

————. "The Objective Bases of Max Weber's Ideal Types." *History and Theory* 16 (October 1979): 265–80.

McLemore, Leland. "Max Weber's Defense of Historical Inquiry." *History and Theory* 23 (October 1984): 277–95.

Merquior, J. G. *Rousseau and Weber: Two Studies in the Theory of Legitimacy.* Boston, MA: Routledge and Kegan Paul, 1980.

Mommsen, Wolfgang Justus. *The Age of Bureaucracy: Perspectives on the Political Sociology of Max Weber.* Oxford: Blackwell, 1974.

————. *Max Weber and German Politics, 1890–1920.* Chicago: University of Chicago Press, 1984.

Mommsen, Wolfgang J., and Jürgen Osterhammel, eds. *Max Weber and His Contemporaries.* London: German Historical Institute, 1987.

Moon, Donald J. "Understanding and Explanation in Social Science: On Runciman's Critique of Weber." *Political Theory* 5 (2 May 1977): 183–98.

Nelson, Benjamin. "Weber's Protestant Ethic: Its Origins, Wanderings, and Foreseeable Futures." In Charles Y. Glock and Phillip E. Hammond, eds., *Beyond the Classics? Essays in the Scientific Study of Religion.* New York: Harper and Row, 1973.

Oakes, Guy. "The Verstehen Thesis and the Foundations of Max Weber's Methodology." *History and Theory* 16 (September 1977): 11–29.

Owen, David. *Maturity and Modernity: Nietzsche, Weber, Foucault and the Ambivalence of Reason.* London and New York: Routledge, 1994.

Portis, Edward. *Max Weber and Political Commitment.* Philadelphia: Temple University Press, 1986.

Ringer, Fritz. *The Decline of the German Mandarins, 1890–1933.* Cambridge, MA: Harvard University Press, 1969.

Runciman, Walter Garrison. *A Critique of Max Weber's Philosophy of Social Science.* London: Cambridge University Press, 1972.

————. "Weber's Understanding: A Reply to J. Donald Moon." *Political Theory* 5 (May 1977): 199–204.

Scaff, Lawrence. *Fleeing the Iron Cage.* Berkeley: University of California Press, 1989.

Schluchter, Wolfgang. *The Rise of Western Rationalism: Max Weber's Developmental History.* Translated and with an introduction by Günther Roth. Berkeley and Los Angeles: University of California Press, 1981.

Shafir, Gershon. "Interpretative Sociology and the Philosophy of Praxis: Comparing Max Weber and Antonio Gramsci." *Praxis International* 5 (April 1985): 63–74.

Slagstad, Rune. "Liberal Constitutionalism and Its Critics: Carl Schmitt and Max Weber." In Jon Elster and Rune Slagstad, eds., *Constitutionalism and Democracy*, pp. 102–29. New York: Cambridge University Press, 1993.

Stammer, Otto. *Max Weber and Sociology Today*. Oxford: Blackwell, 1975.

Strong, Tracy B. "Love, Passion, and Maturity: Nietzsche and Weber on Morality and Politics." In John McCormick, ed., *Confronting Mass Democracy and Industrial Technology: Political and Social Thought from Nietzsche to Habermas*, pp. 15–41. Durham, NC: Duke University Press, 2002.

———. "Max Weber and the Bourgeoisie." In Asher Horowitz and Terry Maley, eds., *The Barbarism of Reason*, pp. 113–38. Toronto: University of Toronto Press, 1994.

———. "Weber and Freud: Vocation and Self-acknowledgement." *Canadian Journal of Sociology* 10 (Fall 1985): 391–410.

Tenbruck, Friedrich H. "Max Weber and Eduard Meyer." In Wolfgang J. Mommsen and Jürgen Osterhammel, eds., *Max Weber and His Contemporaries*. London: German Historical Institute, 1987.

———. "The Problem of Thematic Unity in the Work of Max Weber." *British Journal of Sociology* 31 (1980): 316–51.

Turner, Bryan S. *For Weber: Essays on the Sociology of Fate*. London and Boston, MA: Routledge and Kegan Paul, 1981.

———. "Marx, Weber, and the Coherence of Capitalism: The Problems of Ideology." In Norbert Wiley, ed., *The Marx-Weber Debate*, pp. 169–204. Newbury Park, CA: Sage, 1987.

Turner, Charles. *Politics and Modernity in the Work of Max Weber*. London: Routledge, 1992.

Turner, Stephen P. *Max Weber and the Dispute over Reason and Value: A Study in Philosophy, Ethics, and Politics*. London: Routledge and Kegan Paul, 1984.

Turner, Stephen, ed. *The Cambridge Companion to Weber*. Cambridge: Cambridge University Press, 2000.

Warren, Mark. "Max Weber's Liberalism for a Nietzschean World." *American Political Science Review* 82 (March 1988): 31–50.

——. "Nietzsche and Weber: When Does Reason Become Power?" In Asher Horowitz and Terry Maley, eds., *The Barbarism of Reason,* pp. 68–98. Toronto: University of Toronto Press, 1994.

Weber, Marianne. *Max Weber: Ein Lebensbild.* Tübingen: Mohr, 1984. Translated as *Max Weber: A Biography* (New York: Wiley, 1975).

Wolin, Sheldon S. "Max Weber, Legitimation, Method, and the Politics of Theory." *Political Theory* 9 (August 1981): 401–24.

Wrong, Dennis Hume, ed. *Max Weber.* Englewood Cliffs, NJ: Prentice-Hall, 1970.

SCIENCE AS A VOCATION

It is your wish that I should talk about "science as a vocation."[1] Now, we political economists possess a certain pedantic streak that I should like to retain. It is expressed in the fact that we always start from external circumstances. In this instance this means starting with the question: What form does science take as a profession in the material sense of the word? In practical terms this amounts nowadays to the question: What is the situation of a graduate student who is intent on an academic career in the university? In order to understand the particular nature of circumstances in Germany it will be helpful to proceed comparatively and to see how matters stand abroad, above all in the United States, which in this respect presents the sharpest possible contrast with us.

As everyone knows, here in Germany the career of a young man who chooses science as a profession normally begins as a "lecturer" [*Privatdozent*]. After consulting with and gaining the approval of a representative of the relevant discipline, he qualifies[2] as a university lecturer on the basis of a book and an examination—something of a formality for the most part—in the presence of the faculty as a whole. He then gives lectures on topics of his own choosing within the limits of the *venia legendi*, his license to teach. For this he

---

[1] The German word *Beruf* has a workaday meaning of "profession" but, rooted as it is in *rufen*, "to call," has strong overtones of "vocation" or "calling." Both meanings are active in Weber's usage, and each has been used here where it seemed appropriate. The term *Wissenschaft* means "science" but can refer to any academic discipline or body of knowledge. Thus not only the social sciences but even literary studies, musicology, or linguistics are all called *Wissenschaft*. I have kept "science" here, even though it may seem strange to the English reader who is accustomed to using it with reference to the natural sciences. But I have also used "scholarship" or "studies" and the adjective "academic" where English usage required it.

[2] This refers to the German *Habilitation*, a second doctorate by dissertation that is usually taken about ten years after the Ph.D. and serves as the springboard to an academic career.

receives no salary, and he is rewarded only with the lecture fees paid by his students.[3] In America an academic career normally begins quite differently, namely, with an appointment as an "assistant." This is similar to what happens in Germany in the large institutes of the natural sciences and medicine, where the second doctorate, which is the formal qualification of a lecturer, is obtained only by a fraction of the assistants, and then often only late in their careers. The difference means in practice that in Germany an academic career is generally based on plutocratic premises. For it is extremely risky for a young scholar without private means to expose himself to the conditions of an academic career. He must be able to survive at least for a number of years without knowing whether he has any prospects of obtaining a position that will enable him to support himself. The United States, in contrast, has a bureaucratic system. A young man receives a salary from the outset—a modest one, to be sure. His salary barely amounts to the wages of a worker one rung above an unskilled laborer. Even so, having a fixed salary, he begins with an apparently secure position. However, as a rule, he can be dismissed, like our assistants, and frequently he must reckon that the authorities will not hesitate to dismiss him if he fails to meet their expectations. What is expected is that he will achieve "full houses." This cannot happen to a German *Privatdozent*. Once you have him, there is no getting rid of him. It is true that he has no "rights." But he does have the understandable expectation that if he has worked for years on end he has a kind of moral claim to consideration. This includes being considered—and this is frequently important—in the context of the possible appointment of other lecturers. This raises the question of whether on principle every competent scholar should be allowed to qualify, or whether "teaching needs" should be taken into account. Since this effectively gives the existing lecturers a teaching monopoly, a painful dilemma arises that is closely related to the dual aspect of the academic profession, which will be discussed shortly. For the most part, the second option is chosen. But that increases the risk that however conscientious he may be subjectively, the relevant department head will end up giving preference to his own students. Personally, I should make it clear that I have

---

[3] German students used to have a *Studienbuch,* a notebook in which they registered the courses they were taking in their field. They then had to pay a fixed fee for each course. For staff on a full salary—that is, professors—these tuition fees were a welcome extra. For the unsalaried *Privatdozent,* these fees were the sole source of income.

always followed the principle that a scholar whom I have supervised for his Ph.D. should apply to *someone else* to study for the second doctorate and thus legitimate himself elsewhere. But as a consequence one of my best students found himself rejected by another university since no one would *believe* that this was my reason.

There is a further difference between America and Germany. This is that in Germany the lecturer is *less* concerned with lecturing than he might wish. He does indeed have the right to lecture on any topic in his discipline. But to make use of that right is thought to show an unseemly lack of respect toward lecturers with greater seniority, and as a rule the "major" lectures are given by the professor as the departmental representative of the discipline while the lecturer makes do with ancillary lectures. The advantage of this is that he can devote his early years to research, even though he may not do so entirely voluntarily.

In America the system is organized on entirely different principles. In his early years the young lecturer is completely overloaded precisely because he is *paid*. In a department of German studies, for example, the full professor will give a three-hour course of lectures a week on, say, Goethe, and that is all, while the junior university assistant will have twelve hours teaching a week, including the duty of drumming the basics of German grammar into students' heads, and he will be happy if he is assigned the task of lecturing on writers up to the rank of, say, Uhland.[4] For the syllabus is prescribed by the departmental authorities and the assistant is as dependent on them as the institute assistant is in Germany.

Now we can see very clearly that the latest developments across broad sectors of the German university system are moving in the same direction as in America. The major institutes of science and medicine are "state-capitalist" enterprises. They cannot be administered without funding on a huge scale. So we see the situation that exists wherever capitalist operations are to be found, namely, the "separation of the worker from the means of production." The worker, in this instance the assistant, is dependent on the resources that are provided by the state. He is as dependent on the institute director, therefore, as an employee in a factory is dependent on his boss—for the institute director believes in good faith that this institute is *his* institute and

---

[4] Ludwig Uhland (1787–1862) was a romantic poet who made his name with ballads and poems in a folk style. He also wrote political poetry with a strongly patriotic emphasis. He was always in the second rank and, while still famous in Weber's day, he is now largely neglected, surviving chiefly in school anthologies.

that it is his to manage. The assistant's situation, then, is as precarious as that of every "quasi-proletarian" existence and as that of an assistant[5] in an American university.

Our German university life is becoming Americanized in very important respects, as is German life in general. I am convinced that this development will continue to spread to disciplines like my own where the artisan is still the owner of his own resources (which amount essentially to the library), just as the old craftsman of the past owned the tools of his trade. This development is in full swing.

Its technical advantages are beyond doubt, as is the case with all capitalist and bureaucratized activities. But the "spirit" that prevails in them is different from the traditional climate of German universities. Both outwardly and inwardly, a vast gulf separates the head of a large capitalist university enterprise of this kind and the average old-style full professor. This applies also to their inner attitude, though I cannot go into that here. Both in essence and appearance, the old *constitution* of the university has become a fiction. What has remained and has even been radically intensified is a feature peculiar to a university *career.* This is the fact that for a lecturer, let alone an assistant, to succeed in rising to the position of a full professor or even the head of an institute is purely a matter of *luck.* Chance is not the only factor, but its influence is quite exceptional. I know of scarcely any other profession on earth where it plays such a crucial role. I feel at liberty to make this claim since I personally owe it to a number of purely chance factors that I was appointed to a full professorship while still very young[6] in a discipline in which people of my own age had undoubtedly achieved more than I. And it is this experience that encourages me to believe that I have developed a keen eye for the undeserved fate of the many whom chance has treated, and continues to treat, in the opposite way and who have failed, for all their abilities, to obtain a position that should rightfully be theirs through this selection process.

That chance, rather than ability, plays such an important role, is not exclusively or even chiefly the product of the human factors that are just as prevalent in the selection process in universities as in any other. It would be unjust to blame personal shortcomings in either faculties or the Ministries of Education for the fact that so many

---

[5] Weber used the English word.

[6] Weber was made a full professor in what was then known as political economy (a social science that focused on the state and its resources) at the University of Freiburg in 1895, when he was only thirty-one.

mediocrities occupy leading positions in our universities. The cause is to be sought instead in the laws governing human cooperation, especially the cooperation of a number of different bodies, in this instance, the proposing faculties and the ministries.[7] By way of comparison we can observe the events that have taken place over many centuries in the course of papal elections: the most important verifiable example of a comparable selection process. It is rare for the cardinal who is said to be the "favorite" to have any prospects of success. As a rule, the second or third candidate on the list is selected. The same may be said of the president of the United States. Only exceptionally does the first-rate, outstanding candidate manage to obtain the "nomination" of the party conventions and subsequently run in the election. Mainly it is the number two or number three man. The Americans have already devised technical sociological expressions for all these categories, and it would be interesting to use these examples to study the laws governing this process of selection through the formation of a collective will. However, we cannot do this today. But these laws also apply to university staff, and what is astonishing is not that mistakes are often made, but that, despite everything, the number of *good* appointments is relatively large. Only where parliaments intervene for *political* reasons, as happens in a number of countries, can we be sure that only safe mediocrities or careerists will have prospects of obtaining appointments. The same thing may be said of countries like Germany, where monarchs interfered for similar reasons and where, at present, revolutionary leaders do likewise.

No university teacher likes dwelling on the discussions that precede the filling of posts, for they are seldom pleasant. And yet I can say that in the numerous cases known to me, the sincere *intention* to reach decisions on purely objective grounds was always present without exception.

For we must make a further attempt at clarification. The fact that chance plays such a major role in deciding academic destinies does not spring from the defects of collective decision-making as a part of the selection process. Every young man who feels he has a vocation as a scholar must be aware that the task awaiting him has a dual aspect. He must be properly qualified not only as a scholar, but also as a teacher. And these two things are by no means identical. A man

---

[7] In Germany professors are civil servants and are still appointed by a procedure in which the faculties submit a shortlist of names to the Ministry of Education, which then makes the final choice.

can be both an outstanding scholar and an execrable teacher. I may remind you of the teaching activities of such men as Helmholtz or Ranke.[8] And these are far from being isolated cases. Now the present situation is that our German universities, especially the smaller ones, are caught up in a ludicrous popularity contest. The local landlords in our university towns celebrate the arrival of the thousandth student with a party but would like to welcome the two thousandth with a torchlight procession. "Crowd-pleasing" appointments in neighboring disciplines have a considerable impact on lecture fees, and we should be quite frank about this. And even if we leave that aside, the number of enrolled students is a statistically tangible proof of success, whereas the qualities of a scholar are imponderable and frequently (and very naturally) a matter of dispute, particularly in the case of bold innovators.

For this reason almost everyone succumbs to the idea that large student numbers are a blessing and a value in their own right. If a lecturer is said to be a bad teacher, this amounts in most cases to an academic death warrant, even if he is the greatest scholar in the world. But the question of whether an academic is a good teacher or a bad one is answered with reference to the frequency with which students honor him with their presence. However, it is also true that the fact that students flock to a teacher is determined largely by purely extraneous factors such as his personality or even his tone of voice—to a degree that might scarcely be thought possible.

After extensive experience and sober reflection on the subject, I have developed a profound distrust of lecture courses that attract large numbers, unavoidable though they may be. Democracy is all very well in its rightful place. In contrast, academic training of the kind that we are supposed to provide in keeping with the German university tradition is a matter of *aristocratic spirit,* and we must be under no illusions about this. On the other hand, it is quite true that perhaps the most challenging pedagogic task of all is to explain scientific problems in such a way as to make them comprehensible to an untrained but receptive mind, and to enable such a person—and this is the only decisive factor for us—to think about them independently. There can be no doubt about this, but it is not student numbers that

---

[8] Hermann Helmholtz (1821–94) was one of the outstanding German scientists of the nineteenth century, notable for his contributions in both physics and physiology. His achievements include the formulation of the principle of the conservation of energy. Leopold von Ranke (1795–1886) was a leading German historian whose search for historical objectivity greatly influenced historiography throughout Europe. Both had chairs in Berlin.

decide whether this task has been accomplished. And—to return to our theme—the art of teaching is a personal gift and does not necessarily coincide with a scholar's qualities as a researcher. Unlike France, however, we have no body comprising the "Immortals" of learning, while in the German tradition the universities are supposed to do justice to both tasks, research and teaching. But whether the talents needed for this can be united in a single individual is a matter of pure chance.

Thus academic life is an utter gamble. When young students come to me to seek advice about qualifying as a lecturer, the responsibility of giving it is scarcely to be borne. Of course, if the student is a Jew, you can only say: *lasciate ogni speranza.*[9] But others, too, must be asked to examine their conscience: Do you believe that you can bear to see one mediocrity after another being promoted over your head year after year, without your becoming embittered and warped? Needless to say, you always receive the same answer: of course, I live only for my "vocation"—but I, at least, have found only a handful of people who have survived this process without injury to their personality.

So much for the external conditions of a scholarly vocation.

But I believe that you really want to hear about something else, about an *inner* vocation for science. At the present time, that inner vocation, in contrast to the external organization of science as a profession, is determined in the first instance by the fact that science has entered a stage of specialization that has no precedent and that will continue for all time. Not just outwardly, but above all inwardly, the position is that only through rigorous specialization can the individual experience the certain satisfaction that he has achieved something perfect in the realm of learning. With every piece of work that strays into neighboring territory, work of the kind that we occasionally undertake and that sociologists, for example, must necessarily produce, we must resign ourselves to the realization that the best we can hope for is to provide the expert with useful *questions* of the sort that he may not easily discover for himself from his own vantage point inside his discipline. Our own work, however, will inevitably remain highly imperfect. Only rigorous specialization can give the scholar the feeling for what may be the one and only time in his entire life, that here he has achieved something that will *last*.

---

[9] *Lasciate ogni speranza [voi ch'entrate]!* (Abandon all hope, [ye who enter here]!), Dante, *Inferno,* canto 3, line 9. This is the inscription on the lintel above the gate of Hell.

Nowadays, a really definitive and valuable achievement is always the product of specialization. And anyone who lacks the ability to don blinkers for once and to convince himself that the destiny of his soul depends upon whether he is right to make precisely this conjecture and no other at this point in his manuscript should keep well away from science. He will never be able to submit to what we may call the "experience" of science. In the absence of this strange intoxication that outsiders greet with a pitying smile, without this passion, this conviction that "millennia had to pass before you were born, and millennia more must wait in silence" to see if your conjecture will be confirmed—without this you do *not* possess this vocation for science and should turn your hand to something else. For nothing has any value for a human being as a human being unless he *can* pursue it with *passion*.

Nevertheless, the fact remains that however genuine and profound such a passion may be, it is a far cry from guaranteeing success. Passion is, of course, a precondition of the decisive factor, namely, "inspiration." Among young people nowadays the idea is very widespread that science has become a question of simple calculation, something produced in laboratories or statistical card indexes, just as "in a factory," with nothing but cold reason and not with the entire "soul." Though of course we should note in passing that for the most part there is very little understanding of what actually goes on in a factory or a laboratory. In both places it is necessary for something, and the right thing at that, to *occur* to people if they are to achieve anything worthwhile.

But inspiration cannot be produced to order. And it has nothing in common with cold calculation. Undoubtedly, calculation, too, is an unavoidable prerequisite. For example, no sociologist, even when advanced in years, should think himself too high and mighty to spend months on end doing tens of thousands of quite trivial sums in his head. You cannot shift the burden entirely to mechanical aids with impunity if you want to achieve anything, and what you do achieve is often little enough. But if you do not have a definite idea about the purpose of your calculation, and if during the calculation nothing "occurs" to you about the implications of the individual answers as they arise, then even that "little" will fail to appear. Normally, inspiration flourishes only on a foundation of very hard work. Not always, of course. The inspiration of an amateur can be as productive scientifically as that of an expert, or even more so. We owe many of our very best methods of tackling problems and our best insights to amateurs. The only difference between an amateur and an expert is, as Helmholtz observed about Robert Mayer,[10] that the amateur lacks a tried and tested method of working. He is therefore mainly not in a position to judge or evaluate or pursue the implications of his inspiration. Inspiration does not do away with the need for work. And for its part, work cannot replace inspiration or force it to appear, any more than passion can. Both work and passion, and especially both *together,* can entice an idea. Ideas come in their own good time, not when we want them. In fact, the best ideas occur to us while smoking a cigar on the sofa, as Ihering[11] says, or during a walk up a gently rising street, as Helmholtz observes of himself with scientific precision, or in some such way. At any rate, ideas come when they are least expected, rather than while you are racking your brains at your desk. But by the same token, they would not have made their appearance if we had not spent many hours pondering at our desks or brooding passionately over the problems facing us.

However that may be, the scholar must resign himself to the element of chance that is involved in every kind of scientific endeavor. It is expressed in the question: Will inspiration come or not? A man may be an outstanding worker and yet never have had a valuable idea of his own. But it is a grave error to imagine that this is true only of science and that in an office, for example, the situation is different from a laboratory. A businessman or a big industrialist without "commercial imagination," that is to say, without inspiration or brilliant ideas will continue his whole life long to be someone who ought rather to be a clerk or a technical official. He will never introduce organizational innovations. It is not at all the case—as academic conceit would have us believe—that inspiration plays a greater role in science than in the solving of the problems of practical life by the modern entrepreneur. And on the other hand, people often fail to recognize that inspiration does not play a smaller part in science than in the realm of art. It is childish to imagine that a mathematician will arrive at any kind of valuable scientific discoveries by sitting at a desk with a ruler or other mechanical tools or calculators. The mathematical imagination of a

---

[10] Robert Mayer (1814–78) was a German doctor who made his name following his observation that in the Tropics the color difference between venous and arterial blood was smaller than in temperate climates. He inferred that the higher temperatures made it unnecessary to convert as much food in order to conserve body heat as in colder latitudes. This led him to develop an influential theory of the equivalence of heat and physical labor.

[11] Rudolph von Ihering (1818–92), jurist and professor at Göttingen from 1872 on.

Weierstrass[12] is, of course, organized very differently both in its meaning and its consequences from that of an artist, and indeed, there is a fundamental difference in quality. But not in terms of the psychological process involved. Both are intoxication (in the sense of Plato's "mania")[13] and "inspiration."

Now, whether someone has scientific inspiration depends on fates that are hidden from us, but also on "talent." It is not least this indisputable truth that has led to a belief that, understandably enough, is particularly popular among young people. Today, that belief has put itself at the service of a number of idols whose shrines are to be found today at every street corner and in every periodical. These idols are "personality" and "experience," and the two are closely connected. The idea is prevalent that experience forms the essence of personality and is an integral part of it. People put themselves through torture in order to "experience" things, for that is an essential part of the proper lifestyle of a "personality," and if they do not succeed they must at the very least try to act as if they possessed this gift of grace. Formerly, this "experience" [*Erlebnis*] was known in German as "sensation" [*Sensation*]. And I believe that the latter term provided a more accurate idea of what "personality" is and means.

Ladies and gentlemen, in the realm of science, the only person to have "personality" is the one who is *wholly devoted to his subject*. And this is true not just of science. We know of no great artist who has ever done anything other than devoted himself to his art and to that alone. Even a personality of Goethe's stature had to pay a price, as far as his art was concerned, for having taken the liberty of trying to turn his "life" into a work of art. And even if you question that this was his aim, you at least have to be Goethe to take that liberty. Moreover, it will surely be admitted that even a man like him, who appears only once in a thousand years, could not emerge from this wholly unscathed. In politics things are no different, but that cannot be discussed here today. Even in the realm of science, however, we may say categorically that if a man appears on the stage as the impresario of the subject to which he devotes himself and if he attempts to legitimate himself by appealing to his "personal experi-

---

[12] Karl Weierstrass (1815–97). He is regarded as one of the founding fathers of modern functional analysis.

[13] For example, in *Phaedrus* 245 where Plato writes, "If a man comes to the door of poetry untouched by the madness of the Muses, believing that technique alone will make him a good poet, he and his sane compositions never reach perfection but are utterly eclipsed by performances of the inspired madman."

ence," this is not enough to turn him into a personality. Nor is it the sign of a personality to go on to ask: How can I show that I am more than just a mere "expert"? How can I manage to prove that I can say something in form or substance, that no one has ever said? This phenomenon has increased massively nowadays and always seems petty. It always diminishes the man who asks such questions instead of allowing his inner dedication to his task and to it alone to raise him to the height and the dignity of the cause he purports to serve. And in this respect, the situation with the artist is no different.

These preconditions of our work are factors that we share with art. But we now find them confronted with a destiny that opens up a vast gulf between science and artistic endeavors. Scientific work is harnessed to the course of *progress*. In the realm of art, however, there is no such thing as progress in that sense. It is untrue that a work of art that is created in an age which has developed new techniques, such as the laws of perspective, is somehow superior in purely artistic terms to a work of art that is innocent of all such techniques and laws. At least, such a work of art is not inferior *as long as* it does justice to its own form and materials, in other words, if it selects and shapes its object in a way that is appropriate even without those laws and techniques. A work of art that truly achieves "fulfillment" will never be surpassed; it will never grow old. The individual can assess its significance for himself personally in different ways. But no one will ever be able to say that a work that achieves genuine "fulfillment" in an artistic sense has been "superseded" by another work that likewise achieves "fulfillment."

Contrast that with the realm of science, where we all know that what we have achieved will be obsolete in ten, twenty, or fifty years. That is the fate, indeed, that is the very *meaning* of scientific work. It is subject to and dedicated to this meaning in quite a specific sense, in contrast to every other element of culture of which the same might be said in general. Every scientific "fulfillment" gives birth to new "questions" and *cries out* to be surpassed and rendered obsolete. Everyone who wishes to serve science has to resign himself to this. The products of science can undoubtedly remain important for a long time, as "objects of pleasure" because of their artistic qualities, or as a means of training others in scientific work. But we must repeat: to be superseded scientifically is not simply our fate but our goal. We cannot work without living in hope that others will advance beyond us. In principle, this progress is infinite.

This brings us to the *problem of the meaning* of science. For it is far from self-evident that a thing that is subject to such a law can itself be meaningful and rational. What is the point of engaging in something that neither comes, nor can come, to an end in reality? Well, for one thing, we may engage in it for purely practical purposes, or technical purposes in a broader sense: namely, to enable us to orient our practical actions by the expectations provided by our scientific experience. All well and good. However, that has meaning only for the practical man. But what is the inner attitude of the scientist himself to his profession? If indeed he bothers to search for one. He maintains that science must be pursued "for its own sake," and not simply so that others can use it to achieve commercial or technical successes, so that they can feed or clothe themselves, make light for themselves, or govern themselves. What meaningful achievement can he hope for from activities that are always doomed to obsolescence? What can justify his readiness to harness himself to this specialized, never-ending enterprise? That question calls for some general reflections.

Scientific progress is a fraction, and indeed the most important fraction, of the process of intellectualization to which we have been subjected for thousands of years and which normally provokes extremely negative reactions nowadays.

Let us begin by making clear what is meant in practice by this intellectual process of rationalization through science and a science-based technology. Does it mean, for example, that each one of us sitting here in this lecture room has a greater knowledge of the conditions determining our lives than an Indian or a Hottentot? Hardly. Unless we happen to be physicists, those of us who travel by streetcar have not the faintest idea how that streetcar works. Nor have we any need to know it. It is enough for us to know that we can "count on" the behavior of the streetcar. We can base our own behavior on it. But we have no idea how to build a streetcar so that it will move. The savage has an incomparably greater knowledge of his tools. When we spend money, I would wager that even if there are political economists present in the lecture room, almost every one of them would have a different answer ready to the question of how money manages things so that you can sometimes buy a lot for it and sometimes only a little. The savage knows how to obtain his daily food and what institutions enable him to do so.

Thus the growing process of intellectualization and rationalization does *not* imply a growing understanding of the conditions under which we live. It means something quite different. It is the knowledge or the conviction that if *only we wished* to understand them we *could* do so at any time. It means that in principle, then, we are not ruled by mysterious, unpredictable forces, but that, on the contrary, we can in principle *control everything by means of calculation*. That in turn means the disenchantment of the world. Unlike the savage for whom such forces existed, we need no longer have recourse to magic in order to control the spirits or pray to them. Instead, technology and calculation achieve our ends. This is the primary meaning of the process of intellectualization.

Let us consider this process of disenchantment that has been at work in Western culture for thousands of years and, in general, let us consider "progress," to which science belongs both as an integral part and a driving force. Can we say that it has any meaning over and above its practical and technical implications? This question has been raised on the level of principle in the works of Leo Tolstoy. He arrived at the problem by a curious route. What he brooded about increasingly was whether or not *death* has a meaning. His answer was that it had no meaning for a civilized person. His reasoning for this was that because the individual civilized life was situated within "progress" and infinity, it could not have an intrinsically meaningful end. For the man caught up in the chain of progress always has a further step in front of him; no one about to die can reach the pinnacle, for that lies beyond him in infinity. Abraham or any other peasant in olden times died "old and fulfilled by life"[14] because he was part of an organic life cycle, because in the evening of his days his life had given him whatever it had to offer and because there were no riddles that he still wanted to solve. Hence he could have "enough" of life. A civilized man, however, who is inserted into a never-ending process by which civilization is enriched with ideas, knowledge, and problems may become "tired of life," but not fulfilled by it. For he can seize hold of only the minutest portion of the new ideas that the life of the mind continually produces, and what remains in his grasp is always merely provisional, never definitive. For this reason death is a meaningless event for him. And because death is meaningless, so, too, is civilized life, since its senseless "progressivity" condemns death to meaninglessness. This idea pervades all of Tolstoy's late novels,[15] and it defines the keynote of art.

How should we respond to this? Does "progress" as such possess a recognizable meaning that goes beyond the technical so that

---

[14] Genesis 25:8.

[15] Weber evidently has such works as *The Death of Ivan Ilyich* (1886) and *Resurrection* (1899) in mind.

devotion to progress can become a meaningful vocation? This question cannot be avoided. But it ceases to be merely a question of a vocation *for* science, in other words, the problem of the meaning of science as a career for the person who chooses it. Instead, it turns into the question of what is the *vocation of science* within the totality of human life? And what is its value?

There is a vast gulf here between past and present. You will recall the marvelous image at the beginning of Book 7 of Plato's *Republic*. He describes there the cavemen in chains with their gaze directed at the wall of rock in front of them. Behind them lies the source of light that they cannot see; they see only the shadows the light casts on the wall, and they strive to discover the relationship between them. Until one of them succeeds in bursting his bonds and he turns around and catches sight of the sun. Blinded, he stumbles around, stammering about what he has seen. The others call him mad. But gradually he learns to look into the light, and his task then is to clamber down to the cavemen and lead them up into the light of day. He is the philosopher, while the sun is the truth of science, which alone does not snatch at illusions and shadows but seeks only true being.

Well, who regards science in this light today? Nowadays, the general feeling, particularly among young people, is the opposite, if anything. The ideas of science appear to be an otherworldly realm of artificial abstractions that strive to capture the blood and sap of real life in their scrawny hands without ever managing to do so. Here in life, however, in what Plato calls the shadow theater on the walls of the cave, we feel the pulse of authentic reality; in science we have derivative, lifeless will-o'-the-wisps and nothing else. How did this turnabout take place? Plato's passionate enthusiasm in the *Republic* is ultimately to be explained by the fact that for the first time the meaning of the *concept* had been consciously discovered, one of the greatest tools of all scientific knowledge. It was Socrates who discovered its implications. He was not alone in this respect. You can find very similar approaches in India to the kind of logic developed by Aristotle. But nowhere was its significance demonstrated with this degree of consciousness. In Greece for the first time there appeared a tool with which you could clamp someone into a logical vise so that he could not escape without admitting either that he knew nothing or that this and nothing else was the truth, the *eternal* truth that would never fade like the actions of the blind men in the cave. That was the tremendous insight of the pupils of Socrates. And it seemed to follow from this that once you had discovered the correct concept for the beautiful, the good, or, let us say, courage, or the soul, or whatever it might be, you would have grasped its true nature. And this appeared to be the key to knowing and to teaching people how to act rightly in life, above all, as citizens. For this was the crucial issue for the Greeks, whose thought was political through and through. And that explains why science was a worthwhile activity.

This discovery by Greek philosophy was now joined during the period of the Renaissance by the second great tool of scientific work. This was rational experiment as a way of controlling experience reliably, without which modern empirical science would be impossible. There had been earlier experiments. For example, physiological experiments had been conducted in India in connection with the ascetic techniques of the Yogi, mathematical experiments for military purposes in ancient Greece, and there had also been experiments in the Middle Ages in such fields as mining. But to have elevated the experiment to the principle of research as such was the achievement of the Renaissance. The pioneers here were the great innovators in the realm of *art,* like Leonardo and his contemporaries. Of particular importance were the musical experimenters of the sixteenth century with their experimental keyboards. Starting from these men, the experiment migrated into science above all through Galileo, and it entered theory with Bacon. After that, it was adopted by the exact sciences in continental universities, beginning with Italy and the Netherlands.

What did science mean to these people on the threshold of modernity? For artistic experimenters like Leonardo and the musical innovators of the sixteenth century, it meant the path to *true* art, and for them this meant the path to true *nature.* Art should be elevated to the rank of a science, and this meant, above all, that the artist should be raised to the rank of a doctor,[16] both socially and in terms of the meaning of his life. That, for instance, was the ambition underlying Leonardo's notebooks. And today? "Science as the path to nature"—that would be blasphemy in the ears of modern youth. No, it is the other way around. Young people today want release from the intellectualism of science in order to return to their own nature and hence to nature as such! And science as the way to art? Criticism is superfluous. But even more was expected of science in the age of the emergence of the exact natural sciences. Remember the statement by Jan Swammerdam: "I bring you the proof of God's

---

[16] That is, the level of a university graduate with a doctorate.

providence in the anatomy of a louse."[17] You can see from this how scientific work conceived of its own task under the (indirect) influence of Protestantism and Puritanism. It thought of science as the way to God. That way was no longer to be discovered by the philosophers with their concepts and deductions. The fact that God could no longer be found where the Middle Ages had looked for him was known to the entire theology of Pietism of the day, Spener above all.[18] God is hidden, his ways are not our ways, his thoughts are not our thoughts. In the exact natural sciences, however, where his works could be experienced physically, people cherished the hope that they would be able to find clues to his intentions for the world.

And today? Apart from the overgrown children who can still be found in the natural sciences, who imagines nowadays that a knowledge of astronomy or biology or physics or chemistry could teach us anything about the *meaning* of the world? How might we even begin to track down such a "meaning," if indeed it exists? If anything at all, the natural sciences are more likely to ensure that the belief *that* the world has a "meaning" will wither at the root! And in particular, what about the idea of science as the path "to God"? Science, which is specifically alien to God? And today no one can really doubt in his heart of hearts that science is alien to God—whether or not he admits it to himself. Release from the rationalism and intellectualism of science is the fundamental premise of life in communion with the divine.

This, or something very like it, is one of the basic slogans that you hear from our young people who are religiously minded or in search of religious experience. And they are in search not just of religious experience, but of experience as such. The only surprising thing is the path they take. This is that the only realm that intellectualism had failed to touch until now, namely, the realm of the irrational, is what is now made conscious and subjected to intellectual scrutiny. For that is what the modern intellectualist romanticism of the irrational amounts to in practice. This method of liberating us

---

[17] Jan Swammerdam (1637–80) was a Dutch naturalist who undertook pioneering studies with the microscope. Among other discoveries, he was the first to observe and describe red blood cells (1658). The quotation here is taken from his *Algemeene Verhandeling van bloedeloose diertjens* (1658) (*The Natural History of Insects*, 1792).

[18] Philip Jakob Spener (1635–1705) was a leading figure of German Pietism. This movement initiated a spiritual renewal of Protestantism through an emphasis on personal improvement and upright conduct, which it held to be the most important manifestations of the Christian faith. It had a profound influence on German religious thought and, more generally, on German literature and culture.

from the intellect brings about the exact opposite of what is envisaged by those who adopt it. Thus a naive optimism had led people to glorify science, or rather the techniques of mastering the problems of life based on science, as the road to *happiness*. But after Nietzsche's annihilating criticism of those "last men" "who have discovered happiness,"[19] I can probably ignore this completely. After all, who believes it—apart from some overgrown children in their professorial chairs or editorial offices?

Let us return to our theme. Given these internal assumptions, what is the meaning of science as a vocation now that all these earlier illusions—"the path to true existence," "the path to true art," "the path to true nature," "the path to the true God," "the path to true happiness"—have been shattered? The simplest reply was given by Tolstoy with his statement, "Science is meaningless because it has no answer to the only questions that matter to us: 'What should we do? How shall we live?'"[20] The fact that science cannot give us this answer is absolutely indisputable. The question is only in what sense does it give "no" answer, and whether or not it might after all prove useful for somebody who is able to ask the right question. People are wont to speak nowadays of a science "without presuppositions." Does such a thing exist? It depends on what is meant by it. Every piece of scientific work presupposes the validity of the rules of logic and method. These are the fundamental ways by which we orient ourselves in the world. Now, there is little to object to in these presuppositions, at least for our particular question. But science further assumes that the knowledge produced by any particular piece

---

[19] "I tell you: one must have chaos in one, to give birth to a dancing star. . . . Alas! The time is coming when man will give birth to no more stars. Alas! The time of the most contemptible man is coming, the man who can no longer despise himself. Behold! I shall show you the *Last Man*. 'What is love? What is creation? What is longing? What is a star?' Thus asks the Last Man and blinks. . . . 'We have discovered Happiness,' say the Last Men and blink." See Nietzsche's *Thus Spoke Zarathustra*, translated by R. J. Hollingdale (Harmondsworth: Penguin, 1969), p. 46. Hollingdale prefers "the Ultimate Man."

[20] It has not been possible to find the definitive source of this quotation. The statement may be derived from Leo Tolstoy, "What Should We Do Then?" in Leo Weiner, trans., *Collected Works* (New York: AMS Press, 1968), vol. 17, pp. 249–89 (chapters 32–7). See note 15 above. More of Tolstoy's criticism of science can be found in Leo Tolstoy, *A Confession* and *What I Believe,* translated by Aylmer Mande (Oxford: Oxford University Press and London: Humphrey Milford, 1938). In Chapter 5 he describes how he is "brought to the verge of suicide" by his inability to discover whether there "is any meaning in my life that the inevitable death awaiting me does not destroy." And he concludes a lengthy discussion with the assertion that science in all its forms is unable to disclose such a meaning (pp. 26–35).

of scientific research should be *important,* in the sense that it should
be "worth knowing." And it is obvious that this is the source of all
our difficulties. For this presupposition cannot be proved by scientific methods. It can only be *interpreted* with reference to its ultimate meaning, which we must accept or reject in accordance with
our own ultimate attitude toward life.

Furthermore, the relationship of scientific research to these presuppositions varies according to their structure. Sciences such as
physics, chemistry, and astronomy presuppose as self-evident that it
is worth knowing the ultimate laws governing cosmic processes
insofar as they can be scientifically construed. Not simply because
this can lead to technical advances, but, if science is supposed to be a
"vocation," "for their own sake." This presupposition cannot itself
be proved. Even less can we show that the world that these laws
describe deserves to exist, that it has a "meaning" and that it is
meaningful to live in it. These sciences do not ask such questions.

Or, take the example of a practical art like modern medicine,
which is so highly developed in scientific terms. The general "presupposition" of medical practice is, to put it trivially, that its task is
to preserve life as such and to reduce suffering as far as possible.
And that is problematic. The doctor uses all his scientific skill to
keep alive a dying man even if he begs to be released from this life,
and even if his relatives wish for, and must wish for, the patient's
death, whether they admit it or not, because his life is worthless,
because they do not begrudge him his release from suffering and
because they find that the expense of maintaining his worthless
existence has become unbearable—he may well be a wretched madman. But the presuppositions of medicine and the penal code prevent the doctor from desisting from his efforts. Whether this life is
valuable and when, medical science does not inquire. All natural scientists provide us with answers to the question: what should we do
if we wish to *make use of technology* to control life? But whether we
wish, or ought, to control it through technology, and whether it ultimately makes any sense to do so, is something that we prefer to
leave open or else to take as a given.

Or consider a discipline like aesthetics and art history. The fact
that works of art exist is a given. Aesthetics seeks to explain the conditions in which they arise. But it does not inquire whether the realm
of art may not in fact be a realm of diabolic magnificence, a kingdom of this world and hence intrinsically inimical to God and, given
its profoundly aristocratic spirit, hostile to human fellowship. It
does not ask whether works of art *should* exist.

Or, again, take jurisprudence. This examines the body of legal thought that has been built partly on logic and partly on practices established by convention. It determines which elements are valid; in other words, it determines *when* specific rules of law and specific modes of interpretation are to be recognized as authoritative. It does not explain *whether* such a thing as law should exist and *whether* these particular rules should be adopted. Jurisprudence can only tell us that if we wish for success, then according to the norms of our legal system the best way to achieve it is to apply this particular rule of law.

Or consider the different branches of cultural history. They teach us how to understand the political, artistic, literary, and social products of culture by examining the conditions that gave rise to them. But they provide no answer to questions about whether these cultural products *deserved* or deserve to exist. Nor do they answer the other question of whether it is worth taking the trouble to get to know them. They assume that we have an interest in using this procedure to establish our membership in the community of "civilized human beings." But whether this is the case in reality is not something they can demonstrate "scientifically," and the fact that they presuppose it does not at all imply that it is self-evident. Because that is far from being the case.

Let us now turn to the disciplines familiar to me, that is to say, sociology, history, economics, and political science, and the branches of philosophy that are concerned with interpreting them. It is often said, and I subscribe to this view, that politics has no place in the lecture room. It has no place there as far as students are concerned. I would, for example, disapprove just as much if pacifist students were to make their appearance in the lecture room of my former colleague Dietrich Schäfer[21] in Berlin, surround the lectern, and make the sort of commotion said to have been created by antipacifist students during a lecture given by Professor Foerster,[22] a man whose

---

[21] Dietrich Schäfer (1845–1929) was a historian who taught at Jena, Breslau, Tübingen, and Heidelberg, as well as Berlin. He was a member of the Pan-German Society, and his nationalist, annexationist views became increasingly strident during World War I. He also advocated the unrestricted use of submarine warfare.

[22] Friedrich Wilhelm Foerster (1869–1966) was an educationist and politician who held chairs in Vienna and Munich. His strongly Christian and pacifist views led him to be highly critical of Prussian and German policies during the nineteenth and twentieth centuries. His pacifist views led to a year's suspension from his post at Munich University in 1916. His reinstatement in 1917 was followed by violent clashes between left-wing and right-wing students. After the war he emigrated to Switzerland.

opinions are in many respects as remote from my own as it is possible to be. But it is likewise true that politics has no place in the lecture room as far as the lecturer is concerned. Least of all if his subject is the academic study of politics. For opinions on issues of practical politics and the academic analysis of political institutions and party policies are two very different things. If you speak about democracy at a public meeting there is no need to make a secret of your personal point of view. On the contrary, you have to take one side or the other explicitly; that is your damned duty. The words you use are not the tools of academic analysis, but a way of winning others over to your political point of view. They are not plowshares to loosen the solid soil of contemplative thought, but swords to be used against your opponents: weapons, in short.

In a lecture room it would be an outrage to make use of language in this way. When we speak of democracy in the course of a lecture, our task is to examine its various forms, to analyze them in order to see how they work, and to establish the consequences of this or that version for people's lives. We should then compare them with nondemocratic political systems. Our aim must be to enable the listener to discover the vantage point from which *he* can judge the matter in the light of *his* own ultimate ideals. But the genuine teacher will take good care not to use his position at the lectern to promote any particular point of view, whether explicitly or by suggestion. For this latter tactic is, of course, the most treacherous approach when it is done in the guise of "allowing the facts to speak for themselves."

Now, why should we not do this? I may start by saying that many highly esteemed colleagues of mine are of the opinion that it is not possible to act in accordance with this self-denying ordinance, and if it were possible it would simply be a cranky notion that were best avoided. Now we cannot provide a university teacher with scientific proof of where his duty lies. All we can demand of him is the intellectual rectitude to realize that we are dealing with two entirely *heterogeneous* problems. On the one hand, we have the establishing of factual knowledge, the determining of mathematical or logical relations or the internal structure of cultural values. On the other, we have answers to questions about the *value* of culture and its individual products, and in addition, questions about how we should *act* in the civilized community and in political organizations. If he then asks why he cannot deal with both sets of problems in the lecture room, we should answer that the prophet and the demagogue have no place at the lectern. We must say to both the prophet and the demagogue: "go out into the street and speak to the public."[23] In other words, speak where what you say can be criticized. In the lecture room, where you sit opposite your listeners, it is for them to keep silent and for the teacher to speak.

I think it irresponsible for a lecturer to exploit a situation in which the students have to attend the class of a teacher for the sake of their future careers but where there is no one present who can respond to him critically. It is irresponsible for such a teacher to fail to provide his listeners, as is his duty, with his knowledge and academic experience, while imposing on them his personal political opinions. No doubt, an individual lecturer will not always be able to suppress his subjective sympathies. He will then have to face the sharpest criticism in the forum of his own conscience. And it proves nothing, for other, purely factual errors are possible and yet they do not amount to a refutation of the idea that his duty is to seek the truth. Furthermore, I reject the idea in the interests of pure science. I am willing to demonstrate from the writings of our historians that whenever an academic introduces his own value judgment, a complete understanding of the facts *comes to an end*. But this goes beyond the limits of the theme of my lecture this evening and would call for lengthy explanations.

I ask only this: suppose that we give a class on the forms of church and the state or on the history of religion to a group that includes a practicing Catholic on the one side, and a Freemason on the other. And if we do, how shall we attempt to persuade them to agree to the same *evaluation*? It is quite impossible. And yet the academic teacher must wish and must demand of himself that he should be of use to both of them through his knowledge and his grasp of method. Now you will have every right to say that even in a factual account of the events leading to the emergence of Christianity, a devout Catholic will never be willing to accept the view of a teacher who does not share his dogmatic preconceptions. That is undoubtedly true! But the difference consists in this. Science, which is without "preconceptions" in the sense that it rejects any religious allegiance, likewise has no knowledge of "miracles" and "revelation." If it did, it would be untrue to its own "preconceptions." The religious believer has knowledge of both. And a science without "preconceptions" expects of the believer no less, but also *no more* than the recognition that *if* the course of events can be explained without recourse to supernatural interventions that must be excluded from an empirical account of

---

[23] Jeremiah 2:2.

the causal factors involved, then it will have to be explained in the way that science attempts to do so. And that is something the believer can do without compromising his faith.

But we may go on to ask whether the achievements of science have no meaning for anyone who is indifferent to facts as such and is interested only in the practical point of view. Perhaps they do after all. To make an initial point: the first task of a competent teacher is to teach his students to acknowledge *inconvenient* facts. By these I mean facts that are *inconvenient* for their own personal political views. Such extremely inconvenient facts exist for every political position, including my own. I believe that when the university teacher makes his listeners accustom themselves to such facts, his achievement is more than merely intellectual. I would be immodest enough to describe it as an "ethical achievement," though this may be too emotive a term for something that is so self-evident.

Up to now, I have spoken only of *practical* reasons for not imposing one's personal opinions on others. But we must go further. There are much deeper reasons that persuade us to rule out the "scientific" advocacy of practical points of view—except, that is, for the discussion of what means to choose in order to achieve an end that has been definitely *agreed*. Such advocacy is senseless in principle because the different value systems of the world are caught up in an insoluble struggle with one another. The elder Mill, whose philosophy I do not otherwise admire, was right on this one point when he said that if you take pure experience as your starting point, you will end up in polytheism. This is to put it superficially and it sounds paradoxical, but it contains some truth. If we know anything, we have rediscovered that something can be sacred not just although it is not beautiful, but *because* and *insofar as* it is not beautiful. Evidence of this can be found in the book of Isaiah, chapter 53, and in Psalm 21.[24] And we know that something can be beautiful not just although it is not good but even in the very aspect that lacks goodness. We have known this ever since Nietzsche, and the same message could be gleaned earlier in the *Fleurs du mal*—as Baudelaire

---

[24] In Isaiah 53 we find *inter alia:* "To whom hath the arm of the Lord been revealed? For he grew up before him as a tender plant, and as a root out of a dry ground; he hath no form nor comeliness; and when we see him, there is no beauty that we should desire him. He was despised, and rejected of men; a man of sorrows, and acquainted with grief; and as one from whom men hide their face he was despised, and we esteemed him not." Psalm 22 (not 21 as in Weber) contains a similar evocation of a man despised and abandoned by God ("My God, my God, why hast thou forsaken me?") but whose faith is intact.

entitled his volume of poems. And it is a truism that something can be true although and because it is neither beautiful nor sacred, nor good. But these are merely the most basic instances of this conflict between the gods of the different systems and values.

I do not know how you would go about deciding "scientifically" between the *value* of French and German culture. Here, too, conflict rages between different gods and it will go on for all time. It is as it was in antiquity before the world had been divested of the magic of its gods and demons, only in a different sense. Just as the Greek would bring a sacrifice at one time to Aphrodite and at another to Apollo, and above all, to the gods of his own city, people do likewise today. Only now the gods have been deprived of the magical and mythical, but inwardly true qualities that gave them such vivid immediacy. These gods and their struggles are ruled over by fate, and certainly not by "science." We cannot go beyond understanding *what* the divine means for this or that system or within this or that system. And this spells the end of any discussion by professors in lecture rooms, although, of course, the great problem of *life* implicit here is far from being exhausted.

But forces other than the holders of university chairs are at work here. What man will take it upon himself to provide a "scientific refutation" of the morality of the Sermon on the Mount, and in particular its dictum "Resist not him that is evil" or the metaphor of turning the other cheek?[25] And yet it is clear that, regarded from a worldly point of view, what is being preached here is an ethics of ignoble conduct. We must choose between the religious dignity that this ethics confers and the human code of honor [*Manneswürde*] that preaches something altogether different, namely, "Resist evil, otherwise you will bear some of the responsibility for its victory." According to his point of view, each individual will think of one as the devil and the other as God, and he has to decide which one is the devil and which the God *for him*. And the same thing holds good for all aspects of life. The awe-inspiring rationalism of a systematic ethical conduct of life that flows from every religious prophecy dethroned this polytheism in favor of the "One thing that is needful."[26] Then, when confronted by the realities of outer and inner life, it found itself forced into the compromises and accommodations that we are all familiar with from the history of Christianity.

---

[25] Matthew 5:39.

[26] Luke 10:42.

Nowadays, however, we have the religion of "everyday life." The numerous gods of yore, divested of their magic and hence assuming the shape of impersonal forces, arise from their graves, strive for power over our lives, and resume their eternal struggle among themselves. But what is so hard for us today, and is hardest of all for the young generation, is to meet the challenge of such an *everyday life*. All chasing after "experience" arises from this weakness. For weakness it is to be unable to look the fate of the age full in the face.

The destiny of our culture, however, is that we shall once again become more clearly conscious of this situation after a millennium in which our allegedly or supposedly exclusive reliance on the glorious pathos of the Christian ethic had blinded us to it.

But enough of these questions that lead us very far afield. For a proportion of our young people would commit a significant error here if they were to respond to all this by saying, "Very well, but the reason we come to lectures is to experience something more than just analyses and statements of fact." The error they are guilty of is that they look to the professor to be something other than he is: they are looking for a *leader* and not a *teacher*. But we are put in front of a class only as *teachers*. These are two different things and we can easily convince ourselves that this is so.

Allow me to take you back to America because it is often possible there to see things in their most basic form. An American boy learns far less than a German boy. Despite the incredible number of examinations he is subjected to, he has not yet become, as far as the *meaning* of his school life is concerned, the sort of person who is absolutely dominated by examinations that we find in Germany. For the bureaucracy that uses the examination certificate as an entry ticket to the rewards of office is still in its infancy there. The young American has no respect for anyone or anything, for any tradition or any office, unless it is the personal achievement of the person concerned. *That* is what the American calls democracy. However distorted the reality may be when compared with this conception of it, it is the conception that counts here. The teacher he sees before him is someone of whom he thinks: this man sells his knowledge and grasp of method for my father's money, just as the woman in the greengrocer's sells cabbage to my mother. And that's the long and the short of it. Admittedly, if the teacher happens to be a soccer star, then he will be regarded as a leader on the soccer field. But if he is not (or has no comparable sporting achievement to his credit), he is a teacher and nothing more, and no young American would dream of letting such a teacher sell him any "worldviews" or rules for the conduct of his life. Now, put like this, we in Germany would reject such ideas. I have deliberately exaggerated here, but we may ask whether this attitude does not after all contain a grain of truth.

Fellow students! You come to our lectures with the expectation that we will be leaders, but you do not say to yourselves beforehand that out of one hundred professors, at least ninety-nine are not only not soccer stars in real life, but neither claim, nor have any right to claim, to be "leaders" of any kind in matters of conduct. Bear in mind that the value of a human being does not depend on whether he has leadership qualities. And in any case, the qualities that make someone an outstanding scholar and academic teacher are not those that create leaders in practical life or, more specifically, in politics. It is pure chance if a lecturer also has these qualities, and it would be very questionable if everyone who stands at the lectern were to feel called upon to claim them for himself. And even more questionable if it were left to every university teacher to act the leader in the lecture room. For the very people who think themselves called upon to be leaders are frequently the least qualified to be so. And, above all, whether they are leaders or not, the situation in the lecture room gives them absolutely no scope for *demonstrating their abilities*. Let the professor who feels himself called upon to advise young people and who enjoys their confidence show what he is made of in his personal relations with students, individually. And if he feels he has a vocation to intervene in the conflict of worldviews and party opinions, let him do so outside in the marketplace of life, in the press, at public meetings, in associations, or wherever he wishes. But it is all too easy for him to display the courage of his convictions in the presence of people who are condemned to silence even though they may well think differently from him.

But if all this is true, you will certainly want to ask what can science achieve positively for our "lives" at a personal and practical level? And this brings us back to the problem of its "vocation." In the first place, of course, science gives us knowledge of the techniques whereby we can control life—both external objects and human actions—through calculation. But, you will say, that is just the situation of the American boy and the woman serving in the greengrocer's. I agree entirely. But second, and this is something the greengrocer's assistant cannot do, science provides methods of thought, the tools of the trade, and the training needed to make use of them. You will perhaps object that this is not vegetables, but equally it is no more than the means by which to procure vegetables. Good, let us leave the matter open for today.

But fortunately, this is not the last word about the achievement of science, and we are in a position to offer you a third contribution, namely, *clarity*. Always assuming that clarity is something we ourselves possess. Insofar as we do, we can make clear to you that in practice we can adopt this or that attitude toward the value problem at issue—I would ask you for simplicity's sake to take examples from social phenomena. *If* you take up this or that attitude, the lessons of science are that you must apply such and such *means* in order to convert your beliefs into a reality. These means may well turn out to be of a kind that you feel compelled to reject. You will then be forced to choose between the end and the inevitable means. Does the end "justify" these means or not? The teacher can demonstrate to you the necessity of this choice. As long as he wishes to remain a teacher, and not turn into a demagogue, he can do no more. Of course, he can say to you that if you wish to achieve this or that end, you will have to put up with certain accompanying consequences that experience tells us are bound to make their appearance. So we are back to the same situation. However, these are all problems that can arise for every technician who will frequently find himself having to choose according to the principle of the lesser evil or what is relatively speaking the best option. Only in his case one principal thing is given, namely, the *end*. And it is precisely this end that is *absent* from our situation as soon as we begin to concern ourselves with "ultimate" questions.

This brings us to the last contribution that science can make in the service of clarity, and at the same time we reach its limits. We can and should tell you that the *meaning* of this or that practical stance can be inferred consistently, and hence also honestly, from this or that ultimate fundamental ideological position. It may be deducible from one position, or from a number—but there are other quite specific philosophies from which it cannot be inferred. To put it metaphorically, if you choose this particular standpoint, you will be serving this particular god and will *give offense to every other god*. For you will necessarily arrive at such-and-such ultimate, internally meaningful *conclusions* if you remain true to yourselves. We may assert this at least in principle. The discipline of philosophy and the discussion of what are ultimately the philosophical bases of the individual disciplines all attempt to achieve this. If we understand the matter correctly (something that must be assumed here) we can compel a person, or at least help him, *to render an account of the ultimate meaning of his own actions*. This seems to me to be no small matter, and can be applied to questions concerning one's own personal life. And if a teacher succeeds in this respect I would be tempted to say that he is acting in the service of "ethical" forces, that is to say, of the duty to foster clarity and a sense of responsibility. I believe that he will be all the more able to achieve this, the more scrupulously he avoids seeking to suggest a particular point of view to his listeners or even impose one on them.

The assumption that I am offering you here is based on a fundamental fact. This is that as long as life is left to itself and is understood in its own terms, it knows only that the conflict between these gods is never-ending. Or, in nonfigurative language, life is about the incompatibility of ultimate *possible* attitudes and hence the inability ever to resolve the conflicts between them. Hence the necessity of *deciding* between them. Whether in these circumstances it is worth anyone's while to choose science as a "vocation" and whether science itself has an objectively worthwhile "vocation" is itself a value judgment about which nothing useful can be said in the lecture room. This is because positively affirming the value of science is the *precondition* of all teaching. I personally answer this question in the affirmative through the very fact of my own work. And moreover, I do so on behalf of the point of view that hates intellectuality as if it were the very devil, a standpoint that modern youth endorses as its own, or at least thinks it does. For we may legitimately say to them [with Goethe], "Reflect, the Devil is old, so become old if you would understand him."[27] That is not meant literally in terms of a birth certificate, but in the sense that if you wish to get the better of this devil, there is no point in running away from him, as so often happens nowadays. Instead, you have to acquire a thorough knowledge of him so as to discover his power and his limitations.

Science today is a profession practiced in specialist *disciplines* in the service of reflection on the self and the knowledge of relationships between facts and not a gift of grace on the part of seers and prophets dispensing sacred goods and revelations. Nor is it part of the meditations of sages and philosophers about the *meaning* of the world. This is of course an ineluctable fact of our historical situation, one from which there is no escape if we remain true to ourselves. And suppose that Tolstoy rises up in you once more and asks, "who if not science will answer the question: what then shall we do and how shall we organize our lives?" Or, to put it in the language we have been using here: "Which of the warring gods shall we serve? Or shall we serve a completely different one, and who might

[27] J. W. von Goethe, *Faust*, part 2, trans. Philip Wayne (Harmondsworth: Penguin, 1959), p. 99, ll. 6817–8.

that be?" In that event, we must reply: only a prophet or a savior. And if there is none or if his gospel is no longer believed, you will certainly not be able to force him to appear on earth by having thousands of professors appear in the guise of privileged or state-employed petty prophets and try to claim his role for themselves in their lecture rooms. If you attempt it, the only thing you will achieve will be that knowledge of a certain crucial fact will never be brought home to the younger generation in its full significance. This fact is that the prophet for whom so many of them yearn simply does *not* exist. I believe that the inner needs of a human being with the "music" of religion in his veins will never be served if the fundamental fact that his fate is to live in an age alien to God and bereft of prophets is hidden from him and others by surrogates in the shape of all these professorial prophets. The integrity of his religious sensibility must surely rise up in rebellion against this.

Now, you will be tempted to ask what we are to make of the fact that there is such a thing as "theology" and of its claims to be a "science." Let us not mince our words. "Theology" and "dogmas" are not indeed universal, but they are by no means confined to Christianity. They exist also in a highly developed form (looking back chronologically) in Islam, Manicheism, Gnosticism, Orphism, Zoroastrianism, Buddhism, the Hindu sects, Taoism, and the Upanishads, and, of course, in Judaism. To be sure, they vary greatly in the extent to which they have been developed systematically. And in contrast to what Judaism, for example, has to show, it is no accident that Western Christianity has not only extended theology more systematically, or has striven to, but that its development has had incomparably greater historical significance. It was the Greek spirit that produced this effect, and all the theology of the West can be traced back to Greece, just as all theology of the East (obviously) goes back to Indian thought.

All theology is the intellectual *rationalization* of sacred religious beliefs. No science is absolutely free of assumptions and none can satisfactorily explain its value to a person who rejects them. But every theology adds a few assumptions that it requires for its work and thus for the justification of its existence. Their meaning and scope vary. We may say that *every* theology, including that of Hinduism, is based on the assumption that the world must have a *meaning*. They go on to ask how we are to interpret this meaning so that it is intellectually conceivable. The position is similar to Kant's epistemology, which proceeded from the assumption that "scientific truth exists and it is *valid*" and then went on to inquire what intellectual assumptions are required for this to be (meaningfully) possible.[28] Or as modern aesthetic philosophers (explicitly, as with Georg von Lukács, or implicitly) proceed from the assumption that "works of art *exist*" and then go on to ask how that is (meaningfully) possible.[29] Admittedly, the theologians do not content themselves as a rule with that assumption (which really belongs to the philosophy of religion). They normally proceed from a further postulate, namely, that specific "revelations" are facts vital for salvation, that is to say, facts without which the meaningful conduct of life is not possible. Therefore, these revelations simply must be believed in. Furthermore, they require you to accept that certain conditions and actions possess the quality of holiness, that is, they supply the basis or at least the elements of a life that is religiously meaningful. They then go on to ask yet again: How can these simply indispensable assumptions be meaningfully interpreted within a view of the universe as a whole? Note that for theology these assumptions lie outside the realm of "science." They are not "knowledge" in the sense ordinarily understood, but a form of "having." Whoever does not "have" them—faith or the other requisites of holiness—will not be able to obtain them with the help of theology, let alone any other branch of science. On the contrary, in every "positive" theology the believer reaches the point where St. Augustine's assertion holds good: "Credo non quod, sed *quia* absurdum est."[30] The talent for this virtuoso achievement of "sacrificing the intellect" is a crucial characteristic of men with positive religion. And the fact that this is so shows that despite (or rather as a result of) the theology (that after all reveals this fact) the tension between the value spheres of "science" and religious salvation cannot be overcome.

Properly speaking, it is only the disciple who makes a sacrifice of the intellect to the prophet, and the believer to the church. But never has a new prophecy come into being because (and I deliberately

---

[28] This quotation has not been identified, but see, for example, "How Is Natural Science Possible?" in Paul Guyer and Paul W. Wood, trans., *The Critique of Pure Reason* (Cambridge: Cambridge University Press, 1997), p. 147.

[29] Georg von Lukács (1885–1971) became a leading Marxist philosopher at the end of World War I. Before that he was a noted literary critic and philosopher of art, associated with a circle around Max Weber. He published two influential books on literature, *Die Seele und die Formen* (1909) (appeared in English as *Soul and Form* [Cambridge, MA: MIT Press, 1974]) and *Theorie des Romans* (1916) (appeared in English as *The Theory of the Novel* [Cambridge, MA: MIT Press, 1971]).

[30] "I believe not what [is absurd], but *because* it is absurd" (generally attributed now to Tertullian [c. 155/60—after 220], rather than St. Augustine).

repeat a metaphor that some have found offensive) many modern intellectuals experience the need to furnish their souls, as it were, with antique objects that have been guaranteed genuine. They then recollect that religion once belonged among these antiques. It is something they do not happen to possess, but by way of a substitute they are ready to play at decorating a private chapel with pictures of the saints that they have picked up in all sorts of places, or to create a surrogate by collecting experiences of all kinds that they endow with the dignity of a mystical sanctity—and which they then hawk around the book markets. This is simply fraud or self-deception. A different phenomenon, on the other hand, is no fraud but very serious and genuine, although sometimes open to self-misinterpretation. This occurs when some of the youth organizations that have quietly grown up during recent years interpret their own human communities in religious, cosmic, or mystical terms. It may well be true that every genuinely fraternal act can be combined with the belief that it contributes something of enduring value to a suprapersonal realm. However, I think it doubtful that such religious interpretations do anything to enhance the worth of purely human relationships. But no more of that here.

Our age is characterized by rationalization and intellectualization, and above all, by the disenchantment of the world. Its resulting fate is that precisely the ultimate and most sublime values have withdrawn from public life. They have retreated either into the abstract realm of mystical life or into the fraternal feelings of personal relations between individuals. It is no accident that our greatest art is intimate rather than monumental. Nor is it a matter of chance that today it is only in the smallest groups, between individual human beings, pianissimo, that you find the pulsing beat that in bygone days heralded the prophetic spirit that swept through great communities like a firestorm and welded them together. If we attempt artificially to "invent" a sense of monumental art, this leads only to wretched monstrosities of the kind we have seen in the many artistic works of the last twenty years. If we attempt to construct new religious movements without a new, authentic prophecy, this only gives rise to something equally monstrous in terms of inner experience, which can only have an even more dire effect. And academic prophecies can only ever produce fanatical sects, but never a genuine community. To anyone who is unable to endure the fate of the age like a man we must say that he should return to the welcoming and merciful embrace of the old churches—simply, silently, and without any of the usual public bluster of the renegade. They will surely not make it hard for him.

In the process, he will inevitably be forced to make a "sacrifice of the intellect," one way or the other. We shall not bear him a grudge if he can really do it. For such a sacrifice of the intellect in favor of an unconditional religious commitment is one thing.

But morally, it is a very different thing if one shirks his straightforward duty to preserve his intellectual integrity. This is what happens when he lacks the courage to make up his mind about his ultimate standpoint but instead resorts to feeble equivocation in order to make his duty less onerous. And that embracing of religion also ranks higher to my mind than the professorial prophecy that forgets that the only morality that exists in a lecture room is that of plain intellectual integrity. This integrity enjoins us to be mindful that for all those multitudes today who are waiting for new prophets and saviors, the situation is the same as we can hear from that beautiful song of the Edomite watchman during the exile that was included in the book of Isaiah. "One calleth to me out of Seir, Watchman, what of the night? what of the night? The watchman said, Even if the morning cometh, it is still night: if ye inquire already, ye will come again and inquire once more."[31] The people to whom this was said have inquired and waited for much longer than two thousand years, and we are familiar with its deeply distressing fate. From it we should draw the moral that longing and waiting is not enough and that we must act differently. We must go about our work and meet "the challenges of the day"—both in our human relations and our vocation.[32] But that moral is simple and straightforward if each person finds and obeys the daemon[33] that holds the threads of *his* life.

---

[31] Isaiah 21:11–12. The translation given in the text is a direct translation from Martin Luther's German, of which Weber's text gives a slight paraphrase. This diverges from the traditional English renderings, which arguably may puzzle the lay reader and fail to make Weber's reason for quoting it clear. Thus, the Revised Version has: "The watchman said, The morning cometh, and also the night: if ye will inquire, inquire ye: turn ye, come."

[32] The quotation is from Goethe, *Wilhelm Meisters Wanderjahre,* which contains the exchange, "What is your duty? The challenge of the day." *Weimarer Ausgabe* (Weimar, 1907), vol. 42, section 2, p. 187.

[33] Weber uses the word *Dämon,* which means both "daemon" and "demon." A "daemon" is an inner or attendant spirit. The term goes back at least to Socrates in the *Symposium,* but it was given currency among the educated German public by a poem by Goethe with the title *Dämon,* which was obviously known to Weber and contains *inter alia* the lines: "Even as the sun and planets stood, to salute one another on the day you entered the world—even so you began straightaway to grow and have continued to do so, according to the law that prevailed over your beginning. It is thus that you must be, you cannot escape yourself. . . ."

POLITICS AS A VOCATION

The lecture I shall give in response to your wishes will necessarily frustrate you in a number of ways. In a talk about politics as a vocation[1] you will naturally expect to hear my opinions on topical questions. But I shall say something about these only toward the end of my lecture, and then in a purely formal way, in connection with specific questions about the significance of political action in the context of our conduct of life in general. What will have to be completely ignored in the present talk will be all questions about *the kind* of politics that should be pursued, that is to say, the specific *policies* [*Inhalte*] that *should* be adopted in the course of our political activities. For such matters have no connection with the general question of what politics is as a vocation and what it can mean. This brings us directly to our subject.

What do we mean by politics?[2] The concept is extremely broad and includes every kind of independent *leadership* activity. We can speak of the foreign exchange policies of the banks, the interest rate policy of the *Reichsbank,* the politics of a trade union in a strike; we can speak of educational policy in a town or village community, the policies of the board of management of an association, and even of the political maneuverings [*Politik*] of a shrewd wife seeking to influence her husband. Needless to say, this concept is far too broad for us to consider this evening. Today we shall consider only the leadership, or the exercise of influence on the leadership, of a *political* organization, in other words a *state*.

But looking at the question through the eyes of a sociologist, what is a "political" organization? What is a "state"? A state, too,

---

[1] The German word *Beruf* has a workaday meaning of "profession" but, rooted as it is in *rufen,* "to call," has strong overtones of "vocation" or "calling." Both meanings are active in Weber's usage, and each has been used here where it seemed appropriate.

[2] *Politik* in German means both politics and policy. Here again the choice of word is determined by the context.

cannot be defined sociologically by enumerating its activities. There is almost no task that a political organization has not undertaken at one time or another; but by the same token there are no tasks of which we could say that they were always, let alone *exclusively,* proper to the organizations that we call political, and nowadays refer to as states, or that historically were the forerunners of the modern state. It is rather the case that in the final analysis the modern state can be defined only sociologically by the specific *means* that are peculiar to it, as to every political organization: namely, physical violence. "Every state is based on force," Trotsky remarked at Brest-Litovsk.[3] That is indeed the case. If there existed only societies in which violence was unknown as a means, *then* the concept of the "state" would disappear; *in that event* what would have emerged is what, in this specific meaning of the word, we might call "anarchy." Violence is, of course, not the normal or the only means available to the state. That is undeniable. But it is the means specific to the state. And the relationship of the state to violence is particularly close at the present time. In the past the use of physical violence by widely differing organizations—starting with the clan—was completely normal. Nowadays, in contrast, we must say that the state is the form of human community that (successfully) lays claim to the *monopoly of legitimate physical violence* within a particular territory—and this idea of "territory" is an essential defining feature. For what is specific to the present is that all other organizations or individuals can assert the right to use physical violence only insofar as the *state* permits them to do so. The state is regarded as the sole source of the "right" to use violence. Hence, what "politics" means for us is to strive for a share of power or to influence the distribution of power, whether between states or between the groups of people contained within a state.

This corresponds in all essentials to common parlance. When we say that a question is "political," that a minister or official is "political," or that a decision has been made on "political" grounds, we always mean the same thing. This is that the interests involved in the distribution or preservation of power, or a shift in power, play a decisive role in resolving that question, or in influencing that decision or defining the sphere of activity of the official concerned. Whoever is active in politics strives for power, either power as a means in the service of other goals, whether idealistic or selfish, or power "for

---

[3] That is to say, during the negotiations with Germany early in 1918 that led to the withdrawal of Russia from World War I.

its own sake," in other words, so as to enjoy the feeling of prestige that it confers.

Like the political organizations that preceded it historically, the state represents a relationship in which people *rule over* other people. This relationship is based on the legitimate use of force (that is to say, force that is perceived as legitimate). If the state is to survive, those who are ruled over must always *acquiesce* in the authority that is claimed by the rulers of the day. When do they do so and why? By what internal reasons is this rule justified, and on what external supports is it based?

To start with the internal justifications: there are in principle three grounds that *legitimate* any rule. First, the authority of "the eternal past," of *custom,* sanctified by a validity that extends back into the mists of time and is perpetuated by habit. This is "traditional" rule, as exercised by patriarchs and patrimonial rulers of the old style. Second, there is the authority of the extraordinary, personal *gift of grace* or charisma, that is, the wholly personal devotion to, and a personal trust in, the revelations, heroism, or other leadership qualities of an individual. This is "charismatic" rule of the kind practiced by prophets or—in the political sphere—the elected warlord or the ruler chosen by popular vote, the great demagogue, and the leaders of political parties. Lastly, there is rule by virtue of "legality," by virtue of the belief in the validity of legal *statutes* and practical "competence" based on rational rules. This type of rule is based on a person's willingness to carry out statutory duties obediently. Rule of this kind is to be found in the modern "servant of the state" and all those agents of power who resemble him in this respect.

It is quite obvious that in reality this compliance is the product of interests of the most varied kinds, but chiefly of hope and fear. This includes fear of the vengeance of magic powers or of the ruler, and hope of a reward in this world or the next. More about this in a moment. But when we inquire into the grounds of the "legitimacy" of this compliance, what we discover is these three "pure" types. These ideas of legitimation and their internal justification are of considerable importance for the structure of rule. Admittedly, these types rarely occur in their pure form in reality. But it is not possible today to enter into a discussion of the highly complex variations, transitional forms, and combinations of these pure types. All that belongs to the problem of "general political theory."

What interests us here above all is the second of these types: rule based on the acquiescence of those who submit to the purely personal "charisma" of the "leader." For this is where we discover the root of the idea of "vocation" in its highest form. Submission to the charisma of the prophet or warlord or of the great demagogues of the assemblies, the *ekklesia*, of ancient Greece or of Parliament means that such men are held to be the inwardly "chosen" leaders of humankind. People do not submit to them because of any customs or statutes, but because they believe in them. Such a leader does indeed live for his cause and "strives to create his work,"[4] if he is anything more than a narrow-minded and vain upstart, a passing product of his age. But the devotion of his followers, that is, his disciples and liegemen, or his entirely personal band of supporters, is directed toward his person and his qualities. Leadership has manifested itself in all parts of the globe and throughout history in the shape of two dominant figures of the past: the magician and prophet on the one hand, and the chosen warlord, gang leader, and *condottiere* on the other. What is peculiar to the Western world, however, is something of greater concern to us: *political* leadership in the shape, first, of the free "demagogue" who emerged in the city-state, a political form confined to the West, and in particular to the Mediterranean world, and then, following him, the parliamentary "party leader" who grew up in the constitutional state, an institution that is likewise unique to the West.

These men are politicians by virtue of their "calling" in the deepest meaning of the word. But of course in no country are they the only influential figures in the machinery of political power struggles. What is decisive is, rather, the kind of resources that they have at their disposal. How do the ruling powers set about the task of asserting their dominant position? This question holds good for rule of every kind, and hence also for political rule in all its forms: for the traditional type, as well as for legal and charismatic rule.

Every ruling apparatus that calls for continuous administration has two prerequisites. On the one hand, it requires that human action should be predisposed to obedience toward the rulers who claim to be the agents of legitimate force. On the other hand, thanks to this obedience, the rulers should have at their disposal the material resources necessary to make use of physical force where required, in other words, the administrative personnel and the material resources of administration.

Like any other apparatus, the administrative personnel that constitutes the external form of the political ruling apparatus are not

---

[4] This is effectively a quotation from Nietzsche: "My suffering and my pity—what of them! For do I aspire after *happiness*? I aspire after my *work*!" *Thus Spoke Zarathustra,* translated by R. J. Hollingdale (Harmondsworth: Penguin, 1969), p. 336.

just bound in their obedience to the ruling powers by the idea of legitimacy of which we have just spoken. It is bound equally by two other factors that appeal to personal interest: material reward and social prestige. The fiefs of vassals, the livings granted to patrimonial officials, the salaries of modern civil servants—knightly honor, the privileges of the estates, the status of the official—these are the rewards, and it is the fear of losing them that cements the ultimate and decisive foundation of the solidarity that exists between the administrative personnel and the ruling powers. The same thing holds true for charismatic leadership: glory in war and booty for the military, while the followers of the demagogue look for "spoils,"[5] namely, the license to exploit the ruled through the monopoly of public offices, profits to reward their political loyalty, and prizes to flatter their vanity.

In order to maintain any rule by force, certain external, material goods are required, just as much as in a business enterprise. All forms of state can be divided into two categories. The first is based on the principle that the staff on whose obedience the ruler depends—officials or whatever else they may be—own their *own* means of administration, whether these consist of money, buildings, the materials of war, vehicle pools, horses, or whatever. The alternative is for the administrative staff to be "separated" from the tools of administration in just the same way as the white-collar worker and the proletarian are "separated" from the material means of production in a capitalist enterprise today. The question is, then, whether the ruler has *control* over the administration *himself* and administers matters through personal servants or officials in his employ or personal favorites and confidants, in short, people who are not owners, that is to say, who do not possess in their own right any of the material means of production, but who work under their master's direction—or whether the opposite is the case. This distinction runs through all administrative organizations of the past.

We shall call a political organization in which the material means of administration are wholly or partly under the autonomous control of a dependent administrative staff an "organization subdivided into estates" [*ständisch gegliedert*]. The vassal in a feudal organization, for example, paid for the administrative and legal costs of the fief entrusted to him out of his own pocket. He also paid for the equipment and provisioning needed for a war; his subvassals did likewise. This naturally had consequences for the lord's authority,

---

[5] Weber used the English word.

for that authority was based exclusively on personal fealty and on the fact that the feudal tenure and the vassal's social status derived their "legitimacy" from the lord.

But everywhere, as far back as the earliest political organizations, we also find the lord exercising direct control himself. He seeks to take control of the administration through personal dependents: slaves, household officials, servants, personal "favorites," and beneficiaries remunerated in money or in kind from his own storerooms. He seeks to defray his costs from his own pocket, out of the revenues from his patrimonial estates; and he seeks to create an army that depends solely on himself because it has been equipped and provisioned from his own granaries, storerooms, and armories. Thus in a society based on "estates," the lord governs with the assistance of an autonomous "aristocracy," that is to say, he shares the rule with them. In this second case he relies either on members of his household or else on plebeians, men from strata of society without either property or honor of their own, men who are dependent upon him entirely for their material well-being, since they have no power at their disposal to compete with his. All forms of patriarchal and patrimonial[6] rule, the despotism of the sultans, and the bureaucratic state are of this type. This applies particularly to the bureaucratic state, that is to say, the type of organization that in its most rational form is specifically characteristic of the modern state.

The modern state begins to develop wherever the monarch sets in train the process of dispossessing the autonomous, "private" agents of administrative power who exist in parallel to him, that is to say, all the independent owners of the materials of war and the administration, financial resources, and politically useful goods of every kind. The entire process provides a perfect analogy to the development of a capitalist enterprise through the gradual expropriation of the independent producers. We end up with a situation in which in the modern state control of the entire political means of production is concentrated in a single culminating point so that not a single official is left who personally owns the money he spends, or the buildings, supplies, tools, and military equipment that are under his control. In

---

[6] Patriarchal rule, according to Weber, is traditional rule, based originally on the household, in which the patriarch rules without administrative machinery. Such rule is based entirely on personal loyalty. Patrimonialism arises wherever the ruler develops an administration and a military force that, however, are purely the personal instruments of the master. "Sultanism" is seen as an extreme case of patrimonialism. See *Economy and Society* (Berkeley and Los Angeles: University of California Press, 1978), chapter 3, section 7a, pp. 231 ff.; and also chapter 12, pp. 1006 ff.

the modern "state"—and this is an essential element of its definition—the "separation" of the administrative staff, that is, of officials and employees, from the material resources of administration, has been completed. It is at this point that the very latest development emerges, for we now see before our very eyes the attempt to bring about the expropriation of this expropriator of the resources of politics and hence of political power.[7] The revolution has accomplished this at least to the extent that the legally established authorities have been supplanted by leaders who, through usurpation or election, have obtained political power over the personnel and the administrative machinery, and who derive their legitimacy—whether rightly or wrongly is immaterial—from the will of the governed. It is quite another question whether on the basis of this at least ostensible success they have the right to hope for one further achievement. That achievement would be to proceed with the expropriation of businesses within the capitalist economy whose management is organized at its core in accordance with quite different laws from the political administration, despite far-reaching similarities. This is not an issue on which I shall comment today. I shall confine myself to the purely *conceptual* point that the modern state is an institutional form of rule that has successfully fought to create a monopoly of legitimate physical force as a means of government within a particular territory. For this purpose it has concentrated all the material resources of organization in the hands of its leaders. The modern state has expropriated all the autonomous officials of the "estates" who previously controlled such things as of right and has put itself in the shape of its highest representative in their place.

This process of political expropriation has been enacted with varying success in every country of the world. In it there arose, initially in the service of the monarch, the first categories of "professional politicians" in a *second* sense. This consisted of people who, unlike the charismatic leaders, did not wish to become masters themselves, but to enter *into the service* of political masters. In these conflicts they put themselves at the disposal of the monarch and treated the implementation of his policies as a way of earning their own material living, on the one hand, and of acquiring a life's

---

[7] Weber here takes up a phrase from Karl Marx's prediction of the end of capitalist society as a consequence of its own contradictory development. "The monopoly of capital becomes a fetter upon the mode of production, which has sprung up and flourished along with, and under it. . . . The knell of capitalist private property sounds. The expropriators are expropriated." *Capital* (London: Lawrence and Wishart, 1967), vol. 1, p. 763.

ideal on the other. Once again, it is *only* in the Western world that we discover professional politicians of *this* stamp in the service of powers other than just the monarchs. In the past they were their most important instruments of power and of their acts of political expropriation.

Before we take a closer look at this question, let us make the meaning of the existence of such "professional politicians" perfectly clear in all its implications. It is possible to engage in "politics," that is to say, to seek to influence the distribution of power between and within political structures, both as an "occasional" politician and as a part-time or full-time politician, in the same way as with economic activity. We are all "occasional" politicians when we cast our votes or in any similar expression of our will, such as applauding or protesting during a "political" meeting, making a "political" speech, and so on. And for many people this is the extent of their connection with politics. Today, for example, part-time politicians include all the local agents and committee members of political party associations who, as a rule, pursue such activities only as occasion demands and who do not make it the *primary* "task of their lives," either materially or as an ideal. The same thing can be said of the members of councils of state and similar advisory bodies who spring into action only on request. This applies also to broad swathes of our parliamentarians who are only politically active while Parliament is in session. In the past such groups of people were to be found above all among the "estates."

By the "estates" we understand the owners in their own right of the material possessions vital for military or administrative functions, or the exercise of personal seigneurial authority. A major portion of them were far from willing to pass their lives wholly or chiefly, or even more than occasionally, in the service of politics. Instead, they used their seigneurial power to maximize their own rents or profits and became politically active in the service of their political associations only when their overlord or their peers expressly called for it. The same thing may be said of a proportion of the assistants whom the monarch recruited in his struggle to create an independent political organization that would be responsible to himself alone. The household advisers[8] and, going back even

---

[8] The *Räte vom Hause aus* (literally, counselors [based out of] their own homes) was a term used to describe advisers in a number of German territories who did not normally live at court. Instead, they provided their services only when the king's council was convened in their region.

further, a considerable proportion of the monarch's counselors in the "*curia*"[9] and other advisory bodies were of this type.

But, of course, the monarch could not make do with assistants who functioned only part-time or occasionally. He had to try to assemble a staff of assistants consisting of people who were entirely and exclusively devoted to serving him as their *principal* profession. The structure of the emerging dynastic political system depended very crucially on where he found them, as did the entire character of the relevant culture. And the same necessity was enjoined even more powerfully on the political entities that had completely eliminated or strictly confined the royal power and thus constituted themselves politically as (so-called) "free" polities. These polities were "free" not in the sense of freedom from the rule of force, but in the sense of the absence of monarchical power legitimated by tradition (and for the most part sanctified by religion), as the exclusive source of all authority. Historically, such polities had their home in the West, and their nucleus was the city as a political entity. It was in this form that it first appeared in the Mediterranean cultures.

What did the "*full-time*" politicians look like in all these cases?

There are two ways of engaging in politics as a vocation. You can either live "for" politics or "from" politics. These alternatives are not by any means mutually exclusive. On the contrary, as a rule people do both, mentally at least, but for the most part materially, as well. Whoever lives "for" politics makes "this his life" in an *inward* sense. Either he enjoys the naked exercise of the power he possesses or he feeds his inner equilibrium and his self-esteem with the consciousness that by serving a "cause" he gives his own life a *meaning*. In this inner sense, probably every serious person who lives for a cause also lives from it. The distinction, then, refers to a far weightier aspect of the matter: its economic dimension. The people who live "from" politics as a profession are those who seek to make it their permanent source of *income;* those who live "for" politics are those for whom this is not the case.

In a society based on private property, for anyone to be able to live "for" politics in this economic sense, a number of apparently trivial preconditions must be satisfied. Such a person must be economically independent, in normal circumstances, of the income that politics may bring him. This means quite simply that he must be affluent or have a position in private life that affords him an adequate income. This at least is the normal situation. Admittedly, the

---

[9] The *curia regis* or king's court was convened wherever the king was in residence.

followers of a warlord are as incurious about normal economic conditions as are the followers of a revolutionary hero of the street. Both live from booty, robbery, confiscations, levies, the imposition of worthless currencies whose use is obligatory—all of which amount essentially to the same thing. But these are necessarily phenomena that go beyond the everyday world; in the workaday economy only independent means can perform this service. But more than this is required; in addition, a would-be politician must be economically in a position to make himself "available." This means that his sources of income must not require him constantly to devote all or most of his thoughts and energy personally to the task of earning his living. The person who is most readily available in this sense is the *rentier,* that is, a person whose income does not depend on doing any work at all. This applies to the lords of the manor of the past, and large landowners and persons of high rank of the present who derive their income from ground rents—in antiquity and the Middle Ages, there were also rents for slaves or bondsmen. In modern times, it applies also to people who obtain a living from securities or other modern sources of investment income. Neither the worker *nor*—and this is particularly noteworthy—the employer, and *especially* the large-scale modern employer, is able to absent himself from his work in this way. The employer in particular is tied to his business and *cannot* easily take time off. This is true especially of the industrial businessman, far more than of the big agricultural employer, in view of the seasonal nature of farming. It is mostly very difficult for the businessman to find a substitute, even on a temporary basis. The same thing applies, for example, to doctors, and the more eminent and the busier they are, the harder it is for them to take leave of absence from work. It is easier for the lawyer if only for purely technical reasons arising from the nature of his work, and this explains why lawyers have often played an incomparably greater and even dominant role as professional politicians. We have no need to pursue this line of argument further, but should make clear some of its implications.

Where a state or a party is governed by people who (in the economic sense of the word) live exclusively for politics and not from politics, this necessarily implies that the leading political strata must be recruited on the basis of a "plutocratic" policy. This is not of course to assert the opposite, namely, that the existence of a plutocratic leadership *exempts* the politically dominant class from also striving to live "from" politics, that is to say, to exploit its political dominance for the sake of its own private economic interests. There can be no question of that. There has never been a social stratum that has failed to exploit its position in one way or another. It means only that professional politicians are not directly compelled to seek remuneration *for* their political services as everyone without means is forced to do. But by the same token, this is not to suggest that politicians with no independent means entered politics solely or even principally with an eye to providing for their own material welfare, or that their concern for their "cause" was not uppermost in their minds, or even present at all. Nothing could be more mistaken. Experience tells us that consciously or unconsciously, the concern of the well-to-do man for the economic "security" of his own existence is a cardinal issue for the entire conduct of his life. A ruthless and unconditioned political idealism is to be found, if not exclusively, then at least for preference, in the strata that own nothing, and who because of that fact stand outside the circle of those who have an interest in maintaining the economic order of a given society. This applies with particular force to exceptional, in other words, revolutionary, epochs. Instead, it means only that to recruit politically interested people, both leaders and their followers, *non*-plutocratically, is based on the self-evident assumption that these interested parties can extract a regular and reliable income from the practice of politics.

Politics can either be conducted on an "honorary" basis and thus by what are normally called "independent," that is, well-to-do people, above all, people with unearned income. Alternatively, the leadership can be opened up to those who own nothing and who must then be recompensed. The professional politician who lives *from* politics can be a pure "beneficiary" [*Pfründner*] or a salaried "official." He either derives an income from fees and perquisites for specific services—tips and bribes are merely an irregular and formally illegal variant of this income category—or else he receives fixed benefits in kind or a salary in cash form, or a combination of the two. He may assume the character of an "entrepreneur," like the *condottiere* or the owner of a leased or purchased office in the past, or like the American boss[10] who regards his expenses as a capital investment from which he obtains a return by exploiting his influence. Alternatively, he can draw a fixed wage, like an editor or a party secretary or a modern minister or party official. In the past, fiefs, gifts of land, benefices of every kind, and particularly, with the growth of the money economy, perquisites formed the typical remuneration bestowed on their followers by rulers, victorious conquerors, or successful party

---

[10] Weber used the English word, here and elsewhere in this essay.

chiefs. Today, the rewards that are handed out by the party leaders in return for loyal services consist of offices of every kind in parties, newspapers, cooperatives, health insurance companies, municipalities, and states. *All* party struggles are conflicts not just for concrete goals, but also and above all for the patronage of office. All conflicts between particularist and centralist aspirations in Germany also revolve above all around the question of which authority will have offices in its gift, whether it be the authorities in Berlin or Munich, Karlsruhe or Dresden. Any loss of influence in the distribution of offices is more keenly felt by the parties than setbacks on matters concerning their political goals.

In France a politically influenced change in prefect[11] was always regarded as a greater upheaval, and it caused more uproar than a modification in the government's program since this had for the most part no more than a verbal significance.

Many parties, above all in America, have ceased to be concerned with the old quarrels about the interpretation of the Constitution and have become purely parties of careerists that readily adapt their substantive programs to improve their chances of catching votes.

In Spain until recently "elections" were fixed from above on the basis of an agreement between the two major parties to take turns governing in order to provide their respective followers with posts. In both the so-called "elections" and the so-called "revolutions" in the Spanish colonies, what was really at stake was the state gravy train in which the victors hoped to be fed.

In Switzerland the parties amicably share the posts on the basis of proportionality, and here in Germany, some of our "revolutionary" draft constitutions, such as the one recently proposed for Baden, even envisaged extending this system to include ministerial posts. They thus treat the state and its offices purely as an agency for distributing bounty.

The Center Party in particular was enthusiastic about this idea and in Baden it even proposed including in its program the proportional distribution of offices according to religious affiliation, without regard to merit. With the growing number of offices resulting from the general process of bureaucratization, they are increasingly in demand as a

---

[11] In the administrative reforms introduced in the wake of the French Revolution, France was divided into *départements* headed by prefects who were appointed for their political reliability. Their duties included the maintenance of order, but also the implementation of government policies locally. They were therefore severely affected by changes of government. In the Third Republic, for example, more than one-third of the prefects were replaced after the elections of 1898.

form of *secure* provision. This trend is strengthening among all the parties and in the eyes of their followers the parties are increasingly regarded as a means to the end of providing such support.

However, an opposing trend is to be found in the development of modern bureaucracy into a specialized, highly qualified, intellectual workforce that has undergone a lengthy preparatory period of training. This workforce has a highly developed sense of professional *honor* with an emphasis on probity. Without that sense of honor the risk of terrible corruption and vulgar philistinism would loom over us like fate. This would even threaten to undermine the purely technical activity of the state apparatus whose importance for the economy has constantly grown and will continue to grow, particularly with the increasing trend toward socialization. In the United States, where a professional civil service with tenure for life was once quite unknown, amateurish administration by politicians on the make brought about a situation in which hundreds of thousands of officials, right down to the local postman, had to be changed as a result of the presidential election. This system has long since been undermined by the Civil Service Reform.[12] This change was made inevitable by the irresistible, purely technical needs of administration.

In Europe the professional bureaucracy with its division of labor into specialized fields of expertise gradually came into being over the course of half a millennium. This process began with the Italian cities and *signorie;*[13] and among the monarchies it was the conquering Norman states who took the lead. The decisive step was triggered in the sphere of the rulers' *finances.* We can see from the administrative reforms of Emperor Maximilian[14] how difficult it was for the officials to oust the ruler from this sphere of activity, even under the

---

[12] The Civil Service Reform to which Weber is referring here was inaugurated by the so-called Pendleton Act of 1883. This began the transition from the spoils system to the merit system. Initially, only about one in ten federal employees were appointed on the basis of examinations.

[13] The *signoria* was a form of government by a lord or despot (*signore*) in the Italian city-states between the middle of the thirteenth and the beginning of the sixteenth centuries, replacing earlier republican institutions. The lord who had usually started in a particular office, such as Captain of the People, sought to extend his authority until it was made permanent and hereditary in his family. Notable examples are the Visconti family in Milan, the Estes in Ferrara, and the Della Scala in Verona. In places that escaped the rule of one lord, the term refers to the ruling body of magistrates, as in Florence.

[14] This was Maximilian I (1459–1519), who became Holy Roman Emperor in 1508. His interest in chivalry was intense; he has been given the epithet of "the last knight" and even wrote a lengthy epic poem of knightly deeds.

pressure of extreme necessity and the threat of Turkish domination.[15] This was all the more remarkable, given that finance was the realm that found it hardest to accommodate the dilettantism of a ruler who at the time was bent primarily on being a model of chivalry. Advances in the techniques of warfare produced the expert officer, while the growing sophistication of the legal process resulted in the emergence of the trained lawyer. In all three areas the skilled official finally triumphed in the more developed states during the sixteenth century. And the rise of princely absolutism at the expense of the estates coincided with the gradual surrender of the ruler's autonomous power to the bureaucratic experts to whom he owed his victory over the estates in the first place.

The rise of the trained *bureaucracy* went hand in hand, albeit in a far less obvious process of transition, with the emergence of the "leading *politicians*." Of course, such influential royal advisers have always existed from time immemorial and in every part of the globe. In the Orient the need to relieve the sultan as far as possible of his personal responsibility for the success of government led to the creation of the typical figure of the "Grand Vizier." In the West diplomacy first became a *consciously* cultivated art during the reign of Charles V, the age of Machiavelli.[16] This took place above all under the influence of the Venetian ambassadors, whose reports were studied with passionate zeal in diplomatic circles. The adepts of this diplomacy had mostly received a humanist education and regarded one another as a trained class of initiates. In this respect they resembled the humanist Chinese statesmen of the last phase of the period of the Warring States.[17]

The need for politics as a *whole*, including domestic policy, to be conducted in a formally unified manner by a leading statesman arose

---

[15] During the reigns of Maximilian and his successor, Charles V, as Holy Roman Emperors, the expansion of the Ottoman Empire to the west reached its high point under the leadership of the Sultan Süleyman I, with the conquest of Hungary and the siege of Vienna in 1529.

[16] Charles V (1500–58) was Holy Roman Emperor from 1530 to 1556. Niccolò Machiavelli (1469–1527) was the celebrated Florentine writer and statesman.

[17] The period of the Warring States (475–221 BC) was an age in which China was split up into six or seven feuding kingdoms. It was one of the most fertile and influential of Chinese history. It not only saw the rise of some of the most important Confucian thinkers, but also witnessed the emergence of some of the political structures and cultural patterns that shaped China over the subsequent 2,000 years. It came to an end in 221 BC when the Qin dynasty established the first unified Chinese empire.

in a decisive and compelling way only as the result of constitutional developments. Up to that point there had always been individuals who had acted as the prince's advisers or rather, in reality, leaders. But initially, the organization of the authorities had taken a different path, even in the most advanced states. The supreme administrative authorities that had emerged were *collegiate*[18] in nature. In theory and also in practice, though to a decreasing extent, their meetings were presided over by the monarch in person. It was he who made the decisions. This collegiate system led to the growth of expert opinions, counteropinions, and reasoned votes on the part of majorities and minorities. As a counterweight to these supreme official authorities, the ruler tended to surround himself with purely personal confidants—the cabinet—whom he delegated to convey his decisions in response to the resolutions of the council of state, or whatever name the supreme state authority went by. By such methods the ruler, who increasingly slipped into the role of a dilettante, sought to escape from the inexorable growth of his officials' expertise and to keep hold of the reins of power. This latent conflict between trained officials and autocratic rule was to be found everywhere.

The situation changed only when the prince was faced with parliaments and the desire of their party leaders for power. However, conditions that were pitched very differently led to what was outwardly the same result—admittedly, with certain distinctions. Wherever the dynasties retained genuine power, as was the case especially in Germany, the monarchs' interests were aligned with those of the officials in *opposition* to the parliament and its claims to power. The officials had an interest in ensuring that the leading posts, that is to say, ministerial posts, should be filled from their ranks, and that these posts should become the goals to which civil servants might legitimately hope to be promoted. For his part, the monarch had an interest in being able to nominate ministers from the ranks of the officials beholden to him in accordance with his own judgment. Both sides, however, had an interest in ensuring that the political leadership should face the parliament with a united and coherent front. This meant the replacement of the collegiate system by a single cabinet leader. In addition, the monarch stood in need of a single responsible individual who could cover for him, and who would be

---

[18] Weber has in mind bodies like the Conseil d'État in France and the Privy Council in England, but also the Councils of Workers and Soldiers of the German revolution after 1918. For Weber's discussion of collegiate bodies, see *Economy and Society,* chapter 3, section 8, pp. 271 ff., and chapter 11, section 12, pp. 994 ff.

both answerable to the parliament and able to confront it, while negotiating with the parties. This was essential if he was to be raised above party conflicts and party attacks.

All these interests came together and exerted pressure in the same direction: the emergence of a single minister to preside over the officials and to provide unified leadership. The trend toward a unified parliamentary power became even stronger where, as in Britain, it gained the upper hand in its struggle with the monarch. In Britain the "cabinet," with a single parliamentary "leader"[19] at its head, became a committee representing the power that was ignored by the official laws, but was in fact the sole decisive political power: the *party* of the day that could command a majority. The official collegiate bodies were as such not the organs of the true ruling power, namely, the party, and could not therefore act as the agents of the real government. If the dominant party was to maintain its power at home and pursue grand policy abroad, it needed an effective organization at its disposal, consisting exclusively of the true leaders of the party and able to deal with business in confidence. In short, it needed a cabinet. At the same time, the party also needed a leader who would be responsible to the public, and above all the parliamentary public, for all decisions, in short, the head of the cabinet. In the shape of parliamentary ministries, this British system was then adopted on the Continent, and only in America and the democracies influenced by it was an entirely different system introduced. In this system the chosen leader of the victorious party was elected directly by the people and placed at the head of an official apparatus nominated by himself; his dependence on the approval of Congress was confined to budgetary and legislative matters.

The growth of politics into an "operation" that required a schooling in the struggle for power and its methods led to a twofold division of public servants as these methods were developed by the modern party system. This division was by no means absolute, but it was clear-cut. There were the professional officials on the one hand and the "political officials" on the other. The "political" officials in the true sense can be recognized outwardly by the ease with which they can be transferred and dismissed at any time or at least temporarily "retired," like the prefects in France and the comparable officials in other countries. This presents a striking contrast to the "independence" of officials in the judiciary. In Britain this class of political officials includes those who, according to long-standing

---

[19] Weber used the English word.

convention, lose their posts with every change of parliamentary majority and hence of the cabinet. This category includes, in particular, officials concerned with the general "administration of home affairs"; and the "political" element in this is above all the task of maintaining "law and order" in the land, in other words, upholding the existing system of rule.

In Prussia the Puttkamer decree[20] laid down that these officials had the duty of "representing government policy" or else having to face disciplinary measures, and like the prefects in France, they were used as an official apparatus with which to influence elections.

Under the German system and in contrast to other countries, most of the "political" officials were of the same quality as all other civil servants, since appointment to these posts likewise depended on university study, specialist examinations, and a fixed period of preparatory service. This specific feature of the professional modern civil service is waived in Germany only for the heads of the political apparatus, namely, the ministers. Under the old regime, a man could become minister of education in Prussia without ever having studied at an institution of higher education, whereas it was possible to become a senior civil servant [*Vortragender Rat*] only after passing the prescribed examinations. Under Althoff,[21] for example, in the Prussian Ministry of Education, it went without saying that the departmental head [*Dezernent*] and senior civil servant was professionally trained and hence infinitely better informed about the real technical problems of his department than his boss. In Britain it was no different. It follows that in dealing with everyday business the civil servant was also the more powerful figure. That was not necessarily absurd. The minister was in fact the representative of the nexus of *political* power; his task was to represent its political norms

---

[20] Robert von Puttkamer (1828–1900), a conservative politician who was Minister for Home Affairs (1881–8) under Bismarck. His decree of January 1882 proclaimed that the emperor was responsible for the direction of government and that civil servants were bound by their oath of allegiance to support that policy. His period of office was notable for the rigor with which he enforced the laws proscribing socialism and the thoroughness with which he ensured that officials with liberal views were excluded from state service.

[21] Friedrich Althoff (1839–1908), was the Prussian Minister of Education from 1897 to 1907 and head of its universities section for fifteen years before that. In this capacity he largely determined the shape of secondary and higher education in Germany in the early twentieth century. While expanding the universities and scientific institutes, he intervened regularly in academic affairs. Weber believed that Althoff had tried to block his appointment to a chair in Freiburg in 1893.

and to apply them to the proposals of his specialized subordinates or else to give his officials the relevant political directives.

It is very similar to the management of a business in the private sector. There the real "sovereign," the shareholders' meeting, has as little influence on the management of the business as does a "nation" ruled by professional officials. And the people of decisive importance for the policy of the business, namely, the "supervisory board" dominated by the banks, only give economic directives and select the administrative personnel, since they do not possess the technical expertise with which to run the business themselves. In this respect the present structure of the revolutionary state does not represent any fundamental innovation. For what one finds there is that complete amateurs have been handed power over the administration simply because they have machine guns in their possession, and they wish for nothing better than to use the trained officials as executive heads and hands.[22] The difficulties of the present system lie elsewhere but need not concern us today.

We shall inquire instead about the typical characteristics of professional politicians, both the "leaders" and their followers. These have undergone changes in the course of time and are very diverse today, as well.

"Professional politicians" developed in the past, as we have seen, in the course of struggles between the rulers and the estates of the nobility, and in these struggles they acted as the servants of the rulers. Let us examine their principal types.

In his struggles with the estates, the ruler sought the assistance of politically exploitable strata who did not form part of the estates. These included, first and foremost, the clergy. This was what happened in India and Indo-China, in Buddhist China and Japan and in Lamaist Mongolia, as well as the Christian lands of the Middle Ages. Technically, this was because the clergy were literate. In all these countries, Brahmans, Buddhist priests, and Lamas were imported, and bishops and priests were employed as political advisers. The aim everywhere was to acquire literate administrators who could be deployed by the emperor or princes or the khan in their struggle with the aristocracy. Members of the clergy, especially if they were celibate, stood outside the hustle and bustle of ordinary

---

[22] During the brief revolutions in Germany in 1918–19, the Councils of Workers and Soldiers permitted the traditional administrative authorities to continue their work but sent trusted representatives into their meetings to oversee what was done, without directly intervening, however.

political and economic interests and, unlike the ruler's vassals, were not exposed to the temptation to compete with him for political power of their own to pass on to their heirs. The cleric was "separated" from the machinery of the ruler's administration by the characteristics of his own status group.

A second stratum of this kind consisted of men of letters with a humanist education. There was a time when men learned to make speeches in Latin and write verses in Greek in order to qualify as political advisers and above all to compose political memoranda on behalf of a ruler. That was the age of the first flowering of the humanist schools and the establishment by the crown of professorial chairs of "poetics." In Germany this phase soon passed without leaving deeper traces politically, although it had a lasting impact on our education system. Matters were different in Eastern Asia. The Chinese mandarin is, or rather, was originally, the approximate equivalent of our Renaissance humanist: a humanist man of letters who was educated and who passed examinations in the literary monuments of the distant past. If you read the diaries of Li Hung-chang,[23] you will find that what he took most pride in was the fact that he wrote poetry and was a good calligrapher. This social stratum, with its conventions derived from Chinese antiquity, has determined the entire fate of China. Our own fate might have been similar if there had been the slightest opportunity for the humanists to impose their influence with equal success.

The third social stratum was the court nobility. Once the rulers had succeeded in depriving the aristocracy of its political power as an estate, they attracted the nobility to the court and enrolled them in their political and diplomatic service. One of the factors in the transformation of our education system in the seventeenth century was that the place of the humanist men of letters in the service of the monarchs was taken by professional politicians drawn from the nobility.

The fourth category was a specifically British phenomenon: this was a patrician class comprising the minor nobility and the urban inhabitants of independent means, known technically as the "gentry."[24] This was a stratum that the monarch had originally attracted

---

[23] Li Hung-chang (1823–1901), a distinguished Chinese statesman who sought to open up China to technology from the West. After the Boxer uprising of 1896–8 against Western influence, he was instrumental in mediating between the imperial court and the Western powers, leading to the treaty that ended the uprising.

[24] Weber used the English word.

in his conflict with the barons and that he put in charge of the offices of "self-government,"[25] only to become increasingly dependent upon them subsequently. This stratum remained in possession of all the offices of local government that it took over gratis in the interests of its own social power. The gentry saved Britain from bureaucratization, the fate of all continental states.

A fifth stratum was peculiar to the West, particularly on the Continent, and it was of crucial importance for its entire political structure. This was the class of university-trained lawyers. Once Roman law had been transformed under the late Roman bureaucratic state, it continued to exert a powerful influence over a long period of time. Nowhere was this more evident than in the circumstance that, in its advance toward the rational state, the revolution of the machinery of politics was undertaken everywhere by trained lawyers. This applied even in Britain, although there the great national guilds of lawyers hampered the introduction of Roman law. Nowhere on earth can we find anything analogous to this. Neither the approaches to rational legal thinking in the Indian Mimamsa[26] school nor the further development in Islam of the legal thinking of antiquity was able to prevent rational legal thought from being stifled by theological ways of thinking. Above all, there was a failure completely to rationalize trial procedure. Three factors were blended together to achieve this rationalization: first, the success with which Italian jurists took over ancient Roman jurisprudence, the product of an entirely unique political system that rose from a city-state to world dominance; second, the *usus modernus,* the modern practice, of the late medieval pandect jurists[27] and canon lawyers; and third, the theories of natural law that had sprung from legal and Christian thought and were subsequently secularized. This legal rationalism had its greatest representatives in the Italian

---

[25] Weber used the English word.

[26] Mimamsa ("reflection," "study") is the name given to the earliest of the six orthodox systems of Indian philosophy. It dates back to c. fourth century BC and involves a rational examination of the sacred Vedic texts but was also applied to the analysis of legal texts. It was a powerful intellectual force and is traditionally credited with the defeat of Buddhism in India.

[27] The *Pandects* or Digests were a compendium of fifty books of Roman civil law made by the order of Emperor Justinian and published in AD 533. Roman law came to Germany in the Middle Ages but did not develop until early in the seventeenth century when lawyers, including specialists in canon law, began to interpret the law more freely and to adapt it to modern needs. It was this development that was referred to as the "*usus modernus pandecticum.*"

podestà,[28] in the royal French jurists who created the formal instruments that enabled the royal power to undermine seigneurial rule, in the canon lawyers and the theologians of the conciliar tradition[29] with their theories of natural law, in the court jurists and learned judges of the continental rulers, in the teachers of natural law in the Netherlands and in the monarchomachs,[30] in the lawyers of the English crown and Parliament, in the *noblesse de robe* of the French *parlements*,[31] and finally, in the lawyers of the period of the [French] Revolution. Without this legal rationalism the emergence of the absolute state is as inconceivable as the Revolution. If you look through the remonstrances of the French *parlements* or the *cahiers*[32] of the French Estates General[33] from the sixteenth century until 1789, you will see everywhere the legal mind at work. And if you look into the professions of the members of the French Convention,[34] you will find there—even though they were elected on the basis of equal suffrage—no more than a single proletarian, a very few bourgeois businessmen,

---

[28] The *podestà* (sometimes translated as "mayor") was an elected official in a commune, normally from the nobility of another locality, and invested with supreme legal authority for a fixed salary and for a set period of time. Weber attached great importance to this institution and its role in the development of Italian law in the Middle Ages. His account of it can be found in *Economy and Society*, chapter 16, section 3, pp. 1273 ff.

[29] The conciliar tradition arose as a response to a crisis in the papacy in the fourteenth and fifteenth centuries. It means that as well as the pope, the councils representing the church as a whole have the authority to establish binding norms for church doctrine.

[30] The term "monarchomach," meaning "fighter against the king" or "king-killer," was introduced by the royalist William Barclay (1543–1608) to describe a group of political thinkers in France who had argued for the restriction of the monarch's powers and the right to resist him. See William Barclay's *De Regno et regali potestate* (Paris, 1600).

[31] The *noblesse de robe* was a hereditary nobility conferred on holders of high judicial or legal office in the sixteenth and seventeenth centuries. The *parlement* was not a parliament in the English sense but a judicial assembly, descended from the *curia regis*, or king's court, from the thirteenth century on.

[32] That is, the *cahiers de doléances* or memoranda of grievances that were drawn up at the time of elections to the Estates General. They were collected up and presented to the king estate by estate.

[33] The Estates General was the legislative body in France until the Revolution of 1789. It provided representation for the three estates of the realm, that is, the nobility, the clergy, and the commons (in practice, the burghers of the towns).

[34] The chief of the revolutionary assemblies that governed France after 1789. It followed the Legislative Assembly in 1792 and culminated in the Reign of Terror, after which it was succeeded in 1795 by the Directory.

but, in contrast, a whole mass of lawyers of every kind without whose participation the specific spirit that animated these radical intellectuals and their proposals would be quite inconceivable. The modern advocate and modern democracy have always been inseparable ever since, while advocates in our sense, as an independent status group, have existed in their turn only in the West. They emerged there under the influence of the gradual rationalization of trial procedure since the Middle Ages, as a development from the spokesman [*Fürsprech*] of the formalistic Germanic legal process.

There is nothing accidental about the importance of lawyers in Western politics since the rise of political parties. Party politics just means politics as engaged in by interested parties; we shall soon see what that means. And to conduct a case effectively on behalf of interested parties is the business of the trained lawyer. In this respect he is the superior of any "official," a lesson we have learned from the superiority of enemy propaganda.[35] Admittedly, a lawyer can emerge victorious in a "bad" case, in other words, a case that only has logically feeble arguments on its side; he triumphs by conducting the case "ably," technically speaking. But it is also true that only a lawyer has the skill to plead a cause that has intrinsically "powerful" arguments in its favor and thus to handle a "good" case "ably." An official acting as a politician all too often turns a "good" case into a "bad" one through his technically "incompetent" pleading. This is something we have learned from painful experience. For politics nowadays is conducted preeminently in public and through the medium of the spoken or written word. Weighing the effect of words lies at the heart of the activity of the lawyer but is remote from the skills of the professional civil servant, who neither is nor should be a demagogue, and if he nevertheless undertakes to assume the role of a demagogue he normally turns out to do it very badly.

Given the nature of his true vocation, the genuine official—and this is crucial for our assessment of our former regime here in Germany—should not be politically active but, above all else, should "administer," *impartially*. This applies also to so-called "political" civil servants, officially at least, as long as there is no threat to "*raison d'état*," that is, the vital interests of the dominant order. *Sine ira et studio*, "without anger or partiality"[36]—that should be the

---

[35] Weber is referring to the propaganda campaign waged during World War I. The allegation that by invading Belgium the Germans had violated international law and the principle of national self-determination proved particularly damaging.

[36] Tacitus, *Annals*, book 1, chapter 1.

official's motto in the performance of his duties. He should therefore abstain from doing what politicians, the leaders as well as followers, must always necessarily do, namely, to *fight*. For taking
sides, struggle, passion—*ira et studium*—are the politician's element, especially the political *leader's. His* activity is subject to an
entirely different principle of *responsibility*, in fact, the very opposite principle to that of the official. When an official receives an
order, his honor lies in his ability to carry it out, on his superior's
responsibility, conscientiously and exactly as if it corresponded to
his own convictions. This remains the case even if the order seems
wrong to him and if, despite his protests, his superior insists on his
compliance. Without this discipline and self-denial, which is ethical
in the highest degree, the entire apparatus would collapse. In contrast, the point of honor of the political leader, that is, the leading
statesman, is that he acts exclusively on his *own* responsibility, a
responsibility that he may not and cannot refuse or shuffle off onto
someone else. It is precisely civil servants of high moral stature who
make bad politicians, in other words, who act irresponsibly from a
political standpoint. We must judge them, therefore, to be ethically
inferior politicians of the kind we in Germany have unfortunately
had time and again in leading positions. That is what we call "government by civil servants" [*Beamtenherrschaft*]. I must make it
clear that it is not my intention to cast a slur on the honor of our
civil service by exposing what are political defects of this system, if
we judge it by its success. But let us return once more to the typol-
ogy of political figures.

Since the founding of the constitutional state, and even more
markedly since the establishment of democracy, the demagogue has
been the typical political leader in the West. The unpleasant connotations of this word should not obscure the fact that it was not
Cleon, but Pericles,[37] who was the first to bear this name. Without
office, or rather as the incumbent of the only elective office of military commander[38] (in contrast to the other offices in ancient democracy, which were filled by casting lots), he presided over the

---

[37] Cleon, an Athenian politician of the fifth century BC, who succeeded Pericles as
"leader of the people" in 427. He had mixed success as a general in the wars
against Sparta but is known for the brutal treatment of his enemies once he had
defeated them. His long-term reputation is that of a conventional vulgar demagogue. Pericles (495–427 BC) was one of the outstanding figures of Athenian
democracy.

[38] Weber uses *Oberstrategen*—"high strategist"—and clearly means what the
Greeks call *strategos*.

sovereign assembly [*ekklesia*] of the people [*demos*] of Athens. Modern demagogues, too, make use of speech, and they do so to a formidable degree, when you consider the election speeches that a modern candidate has to make. But they use the printed word even more. The political publicist, and above all, the *journalist* is the most important representative of the species today.

To provide even an outline of the sociology of modern political journalism would go well beyond the framework of this lecture, since that would be a separate topic in its own right. But a few points must be made. The journalist shares with all demagogues and lawyers (as well as artists) the fate of being denied a fixed place in the social structure. This is true on the Continent, at least, and it contrasts with conditions in Britain and, incidentally, with the situation that formerly obtained in Prussia. He belongs to a kind of pariah caste that in the eyes of "society" is always judged socially by its lowest representatives from the point of view of morality. Hence, the strangest ideas are prevalent about journalists and their work. Not everyone realizes that to write a really *good* piece of journalism is at least as demanding intellectually as the achievement of any scholar. This is particularly true when we recollect that it has to be written on the spot, to order, and that it must create an immediate *effect*, even though it is produced under completely different conditions from that of scholarly research. It is generally overlooked that a journalist's actual responsibility is far greater than a scholar's, and that on average every reputable journalist's *sense* of responsibility is by no means inferior, as indeed we saw during the war. It is overlooked because in the nature of the case it is the *irresponsible* pieces of journalism that tend to remain in the memory because of their often terrible effects. And no one believes it possible for competent journalists to be more discreet on average than other people. And yet it is so. The incomparably greater temptations to which this profession is exposed, together with the other conditions of working as a journalist at the present time, have conditioned the public to regard the press with a mixture of disdain and abject cowardice. It is not possible to discuss today how this might be remedied. What interests us here is the *political* destiny that journalists can aspire to, the opportunities they have to gain positions of leadership in politics. Hitherto, openings occurred only in the Social Democratic Party. However, within the party editorial posts resembled civil service posts for the most part but have not proved to be a springboard to a position in the *leadership*.

In the bourgeois parties the prospects of gaining political power by this route have, if anything, deteriorated on the whole, when compared to the previous generation. Needless to say, every politician of importance has stood in need of press influence and hence also connections with the press. But contrary to what might have been expected, for party *leaders* to emerge from the ranks of the press was very much the exception. The reason for this lies in the journalist's greatly reduced ability to obtain time off from his work. This applies above all to the journalist with no private means since he is necessarily tied to his professional duties. A journalist's duties, moreover, have become much more intensive, as has the importance of being up to date. The need to earn a living by writing articles on a daily or weekly basis is a millstone around the neck of politicians, and I know of some who are leaders by nature but whose rise to power has been outwardly and, even more importantly, inwardly paralyzed by this burden. The fact that under the old regime relations between the press and the ruling powers in the state and in the parties had a dire effect on the quality of journalism is a story in its own right. These relations were different in the countries of our enemies. But even there, and indeed in all modern states, it appears that the political influence of the ordinary working journalist is constantly being eroded, while the influence of the capitalist press magnate, such as "Lord" Northcliffe,[39] grows apace.

Admittedly, in Germany hitherto the great capitalist newspaper concerns have mainly taken over the newspapers with the "small ads," that is, the various "General Advertisers," and as a general rule they have promoted political apathy. For no profits were to be made from an independent line in politics, and such independence was even less likely to earn the commercially helpful goodwill of the ruling political powers. During the war the revenues brought in by advertising could be targeted as a way of exerting political influence on the press, and this practice looks set to continue. Even if the major newspapers can be expected to resist this pressure, the position of the smaller ones is far more precarious. In any case, in Germany at present a journalistic career is not a normal career route for aspiring political leaders. Whether we should add "any longer" or "not yet," we shall perhaps have to wait to see. This is not to discount its other attractions or to deny its opportunities for influencing and changing politics and, above all, the degree of political responsibility it may entail.

---

[39] Alfred, Lord Northcliffe (1865–1922), was a British press lord. He founded papers like the *Daily Mail* (1903) and *Daily Mirror* (1904), rescued the *Observer* (1908), and bought up *The Times*. He worked closely with his younger brother, who became Viscount Rothermere.

Whether the position would change at all if the principle of anonymity were to be abandoned, as some but not all journalists propose, is hard to say. During the war some newspapers in Germany were edited by talented writers who had been specially hired for the purpose and who made a point of writing under their own names. Unfortunately, what we found in a number of the better-known cases was that this approach does *not* necessarily foster the enhanced sense of responsibility that we might have expected. It was in part the most notorious elements of the popular press who, regardless of party allegiance, used this tactic to strive for higher sales—and who did in fact achieve them. This practice undoubtedly increased the wealth of the gentlemen concerned, the publishers as well as the sensation-seeking journalists—but not their *honor.* This does not amount to an argument against the principle; the question is highly complex, and we should not generalize from this one experience.

Hitherto, however, journalism has not proved to be the road to genuine leadership or to the *responsible* conduct of political life. How matters will develop further, only time will tell. Whatever happens, however, a career in journalism will remain one of the most important paths to professional political activity. Not a path for just anybody, however, least of all for people of weak character, especially for people who can maintain their inner equilibrium only where their social and professional status is secure. A young scholar's life involves something of a gamble, but he is at least surrounded by the stable conventions of social status that help to prevent him from going off the rails. A journalist's life, however, is in every sense a gamble pure and simple. Moreover, he works under conditions that subject his inner sense of security to a sterner test than almost any other situation. His often bitter professional disappointments may not even be the worst aspect of this.

Indeed, it is above all the successful journalists who find themselves having to face particularly onerous inner challenges. It is no small thing to consort with the powerful people of this earth in their drawing rooms, apparently on a basis of equality, to be flattered because you are feared, while all the time knowing that no sooner has the door closed behind you than your host may have to defend himself to his guests for having invited the "scoundrels from the press." In the same way, it is no small thing to deliver prompt and yet convincing judgments on anything and everything that the "market" happens to call for, on every conceivable problem of life, without succumbing to absolute superficiality, or what is even worse, to the humiliation of self-exposure with its inexorable consequences.

We should not find it astonishing that so many journalists have gone off the rails or have otherwise lost their value as human beings. What is surprising is that, despite everything, this stratum of society contains a much greater number of valuable and absolutely genuine human beings than outsiders tend to suppose.

As a type of professional politician, the journalist can look back on what is a considerable past. The figure of the *party official,* in contrast, is a phenomenon of recent decades or, in some cases, just the last few years. We must turn our attention to an examination of the party system and party organization if we are to gain an understanding of the historical significance of this figure.

In all political entities of any size where the rulers are elected periodically, that is to say, in all entities that exceed the scope and authority of small, rural cantons, the organization of politics is necessarily an *organization of interested parties.* This means that a relatively small number of people with a primary interest in political activity, that is, in sharing in political power, create a following through open recruitment, offer themselves or their protégés as candidates for election, raise funds, and sally forth in search of votes. It is not possible to imagine how in large organizations elections could take place effectively in the absence of these activities. In practice, it means the division of all enfranchised citizens into politically active and politically passive segments. Since this distinction is voluntary, it cannot be eliminated by such measures as compulsory voting, representation according to membership of a "professional group," or other proposals designed explicitly or in fact to combat this state of affairs and thus do away with the dominance of the professional politicians. Leaders and followers are the indispensable vital components of every party: the leadership so as actively to recruit the followers, while the followers enlist the support of the passive electorate for the election of the leader.

Differences arise, however, in party structure. The "parties" in medieval city-states, the Guelphs and the Ghibellines, for example, had purely personal followings. Consider the *Statuto della parte Guelfa,*[40] with its call for the confiscation of the property of the *nobili* (this term referred originally to all families who lived like knights,

---

[40] The Guelphs and the Ghibellines were the two great factions in Italian politics during the Middle Ages. In the protracted conflicts between the papacy and the Holy Roman Emperors, the Guelphs supported the former and the Ghibellines the latter. After the end of the thirteenth century, these party names came to be used to designate different social classes, especially in the northern and central Italian states. The *Statuto della parte Guelfa* was published in 1335.

that is to say, were entitled to hold a fief), their exclusion from office and the franchise, the party committees linking different localities, the strictly military organizations, and the bonuses paid for denunciations. If we consider these things, we find ourselves strongly reminded of Bolshevism with its Soviets, its strictly screened organization of military personnel, and—above all, in Russia—its armies of informers, its confiscations, and the disarming and political disenfranchisement of its "bourgeois," in other words, its entrepreneurs, tradesmen, *rentiers,* clerics, descendants of the royal dynasty, and police agents.

The analogy is even more striking on closer inspection. On the one hand, you find that the military organization of the Guelph party consisted of a purely knightly army, drawn up on the basis of registered feudal estates, and that almost all its leading positions were filled by the nobility. On the other, the Soviets retained, or rather reintroduced, highly paid entrepreneurs, the piecework system of wages, Taylorism, and discipline in both the armed forces and the workplace, all the while on the lookout for foreign capital. In a word, then, simply in order to keep the state and the economy functioning, they were forced to accept once again absolutely *all* the things they had combated as bourgeois class institutions, and they were forced even to take over, as a principal instrument of their state power, the agents of the old Okhrana.[41] However, we are not dealing here with organizations concerned with force but with professional politicians who strive to gain power through sober, "peaceful" party campaigning in the electoral marketplace.

In the same way, these parties in our ordinary understanding of the word started life, in Britain, for example, as pure followers of the aristocracy. Every time a peer changed sides, for whatever reason, everyone who depended on him changed sides with him. Until the Reform Bill [of 1832] the great aristocratic families, and not least the king himself, controlled the patronage of a vast number of constituencies. Closely associated with these aristocratic parties are the parties of notables of the kind that emerged everywhere with the growth of the power of the bourgeoisie. Under the leadership of the typical strata of intellectuals of the West, the property-owning and educated classes divided into parties, which they led and which were based partly on class interests, partly on family tradition, and partly on pure ideology. Clergymen, teachers, professors, lawyers, doctors,

---

[41] The Okhrana was the secret police department in tsarist Russia. It was replaced in 1917, after the October Revolution, by the Cheka (the Extraordinary Commission [for Combating Counterrevolution, Sabotage, and Speculation]).

pharmacists, wealthy farmers, factory owners—in Britain, an entire stratum whose members called themselves gentlemen—initially formed associations as opportunity offered and at the most established political clubs at the local level. In unsettled times the petty bourgeoisie would speak up, and on occasion even the proletariat found its voice, when it obtained leaders, although these leaders did not, generally speaking, arise from their ranks.

In the country, regionally organized parties on a permanent basis did not yet exist at this stage. It was simply the members of Parliament themselves who kept the parties together. The selection of candidates lay crucially in the hands of the local notables. Party programs came into being partly through the candidates' campaign appeals, partly on the basis of congresses of notables or decisions of the parliamentary party. The clubs were run on a part-time or honorary basis, as occasional work. Where there were no clubs (as was mostly the case), one found nothing but the entirely informal political activity of the few people with a lasting interest in politics in normal times. The journalist alone was a paid professional politician, and only the newspapers were able to act as a continuous form of political organization. Aside from that, there was only Parliament in session. Of course, parliamentarians and parliamentary leaders knew perfectly well which local notables to approach when a specific political course of action was desired. But only large towns had party associations that could count on modest members' contributions, periodic conferences, and public meetings at which the local member of Parliament could report on his activities. Politics came to life only at election time.

The driving force behind the progressive tightening of party organization was the interest that members of Parliament had in the possibility of electoral compromises between localities and the impact of unified programs recognized by broad sections of the public throughout the country, as well as of unified electioneering platforms. But the party apparatus remains that of an association of notables, and no change in principle is involved even when the entire country is covered by a network of local party branches, including medium-sized towns, as well as a set of "party agents" with whom a member of Parliament in charge of the central party bureau is in constant correspondence. There are as yet no paid officials outside the central party headquarters. The affairs of the local branches are still conducted by "reputable" people who take on this task because of the esteem they otherwise enjoy. They are the nonparliamentary "notables" who exert influence alongside the political notables who actually have seats in Parliament. Increasingly, however, the intellectual nourishment of both the press and the local branches is provided by the party correspondence published by the party. Regular members' contributions become indispensable; a fraction of the money received is used to defray the costs of party headquarters. This was the position of the majority of party organizations in Germany until fairly recently.

Even more strikingly, in France the first stage still prevailed in part. By this is meant the whole unstable system of parliamentary alliances, the small number of local notables in the country beyond, programs drafted by the candidates or by their sponsors on their behalf, in some instances at the moment of recruiting them, although with a more or less local interpretation of directives and programs issued by the parliamentarians. This system was only gradually superseded. The number of full-time politicians remained small and consisted chiefly of elected deputies, the few officials in party headquarters, the journalists, and—in France—the careerists who happened to fill a "political post" or were on the lookout for one. Formally, politics was predominantly a part-time profession. Likewise, the number of deputies eligible for ministerial posts was very restricted, and since places were confined to notables, the number of candidates for election was limited, too. However, the number of people with an indirect interest in the conduct of politics, particularly a material interest, was very great. For all measures taken by a ministry, above all everything to do with questions of personnel, could be dealt with only by taking into consideration their influence on the chances of being elected. Thus everyone tried to channel their wishes of any and every kind through the local deputy, and, whether he liked it or not, the minister was forced to listen to him if he belonged to his majority, which was therefore the goal to which everyone aspired. The individual deputy had all offices in his gift, as well as every other kind of patronage within his constituency, and, for his part, he cultivated his own contacts to the local notables so as to ensure his own reelection.

The most modern forms of party organization stand in stark contrast to this idyllic state of affairs dominated by notables and, above all, by the members of Parliament. They are the offspring of democracy, the mass suffrage, the need to woo the masses and for mass organization, the development of the greatest degree of unity in the leadership and the strictest possible discipline. The rule by notables and the control exercised by members of Parliament dies out. "Full-time" politicians *outside* Parliament take the operations of politics into their own hands, either as "entrepreneurs," which is what the

American "boss"[42] and the English "election agent" essentially were, or else as officials on a fixed salary.

In formal terms, a far-reaching process of democratization takes place. It is no longer the parliamentary party that creates the authoritative programs, nor the local notables who still exercise control over the nomination of candidates. Instead, the organized party members meet to choose the candidates and delegate members to attend assemblies at a higher level, of which there may be several, right up to the general "party congress." In the nature of the case, however, power lies in the hands of those who do the *continuous* day-to-day work within the organization or of those on whom the party apparatus depends for either money or personnel, whether as patrons or as the leaders of powerful clubs representing vested interests (such as Tammany Hall). What is crucial is that this entire human apparatus—the party "machine," as it is significantly called in the Anglo-Saxon nations—or rather, the people in charge of it, holds the members of Parliament in check and is well placed to impose its will on them. This has particular importance for the selection of the party *leadership*. You become a leader only if you are supported by the machine, even over the heads of the members of Parliament. The creation of such machines, in other words, signifies the emergence of a *plebiscitary* democracy.

Needless to say, the party followers, particularly the party officials and bosses, look to the victory of their leader for personal reward in the form of offices or other benefits. The crucial point is that they expect to obtain these things from him and not, or not only, from the individual members of Parliament. They expect above all that the demagogic effect of the leader's *personality* in the election campaign will bring the party both votes and seats, and hence power, and that this will improve as far as possible its supporters' chances of obtaining the hoped-for rewards. At the level of ideals, there is the satisfaction of working for a person to whom you are personally devoted and in whom you have faith, instead of merely for the abstract program of a party composed of mediocrities. This is the *charismatic* element in all leadership and one of its mainsprings.

This form ultimately prevailed, though its triumph was uneven and it involved a latent conflict with the local notables and members of Parliament eager to retain their influence. The process could be seen among the bourgeois parties, first of all in the United States, and then in the Social Democratic Party, especially in Germany. There are

---

[42] "Boss" and "election agent" are used in the original.

constant setbacks whenever a universally acknowledged leader fails to appear, and even when there is one, all sorts of concessions have to be made to the vanity and self-interest of the party notables. Above all, however, even the party machine can succumb to the dominance of the party *officials* who control the day-to-day business. Many members of the Social Democratic Party believe that their party has been unable to resist this process of "bureaucratization." However, the fact is that "officials" tend to submit fairly readily to a demagogic leader with a powerful personality. Their ideal and material interests are intimately bound up with what they hope the party will achieve thanks to him, while working for a leader is psychologically more satisfying. It is much more difficult for leaders to emerge where, as in the majority of bourgeois parties, the "notables" exert an influence on party affairs alongside the officials. For in their *minds,* the little posts the notables occupy on the board or the committees come to "constitute their life." Their actions are determined by resentment toward the demagogue as a *homo novus,* an upstart, by their firm belief in the superiority of the "experience" of party politics (which is in fact of considerable importance) and by ideological anxieties that the old party traditions may be at risk. In the party they have all the traditionalist elements on their side. The rural voters, above all, but also voters from the petty bourgeoisie look up to the name of the notable with whom they have long been familiar and mistrust the new man whom they do not know. Nevertheless, *if* the latter proves successful, these voters switch their loyalty and support him all the more steadfastly. Let us consider a few of the chief examples of this conflict between competing political structures and, in particular, the rise of the plebiscitary form as Ostrogorski describes it.[43]

Let us start with Britain: there until 1868 party organization consisted almost entirely of notables.[44] In rural districts, the Tories

---

[43] M. Ostrogorski, *Democracy and the Organization of Political Parties* (London: Macmillan, 1902). Moisei Ostrogorski (1854–1919) was a Russian political scientist and politician. After lengthy periods of study in Britain and the United States in the 1880s and 1890s, he published pioneering works on the history of the political parties. After the revolution of 1905, he returned to Russia and was elected to the First Duma as a liberal. Following the dissolution of the Duma, he withdrew from politics and settled in the United States.

[44] Weber alludes here to Disraeli's Reform Bill of 1867. This more or less doubled the electorate in the towns by reducing the property qualification, enabling some working men to take part in the electoral process for the first time. At the same time it greatly increased the number of constituencies, particularly in the countryside. These measures forced the British parties to adopt tighter forms of organization.

relied on such people as the Anglican vicar, schoolmasters, for the most part, and above all the large landowners of the county. The Whigs looked for their support to such people as nonconformist preachers (where they were to be found), the postmaster, the blacksmith, the tailor, the rope maker, in short, skilled artisans who could exert political influence because it was easy to chat with them. In the towns the parties were divided partly along economic lines, partly on religious ones, or even simply by the political opinions that were handed down through the family. But in all cases the notables were the active agents in the political organizations. Above them, there was Parliament and the parties with the cabinet and the "leader"[45] who either presided over the cabinet or led the opposition. This leader had at his side the most important professional figure in the party organization, namely, the "whip."[46] It was he who had the desirable offices in his gift; it was to him, therefore, that the careerists had to apply. His practice was to come to an understanding with the individual constituency members about such matters. In the constituencies a stratum of professional politicians gradually began to emerge. Local agents were recruited who initially were unpaid and were roughly comparable to our "party agents" [*Vertrauensmänner*] in Germany. Alongside them, however, there developed in the constituencies a form of capitalist entrepreneur known as the "election agent."[47] In modern British legislation, with its emphasis on fairness in the conduct of elections, the appearance of the election agent was unavoidable. This legislation sought to control the costs of elections and to stem the power of money, since it obliged candidates to declare their electoral expenses. For in Britain, to a far greater extent than was the case here in Germany, the candidate had the pleasure of loosening his purse strings, in addition to straining his voice. He had to pay the election agent a lump sum to cover all his expenses and from which the latter normally made a good profit. In Britain, in the distribution of power between the "leader" and the party notables, both in Parliament and in the country, it had always been the leader who had the more significant position. There were compelling reasons for this in the need to make large-scale policy making possible in a consistent manner. Notwithstanding this, the influence of members of Parliament and party notables remained considerable.

---

[45] Weber used the English word.

[46] Weber used the English word.

[47] Weber used the English term.

This, then, is what the old party organization looked like: half a club for notables, half already a business complete with employees and entrepreneurs. From 1868 on, however, we can see the development of the "caucus system,"[48] first for local elections in Birmingham, and then throughout the country. This system was brought into being by a nonconformist parson together with Joseph Chamberlain.[49] What caused it was the democratization of the franchise. In order to win the support of the masses, it was necessary to summon into existence a vast apparatus of organizations that were democratic in appearance. The aim was to create an electoral association in every district of each town, to keep the organization in operation at all times, and to run it strictly on bureaucratic lines. This involved the recruitment of growing numbers of paid officials, while the formal representatives of party policy were leading negotiators with the right to co-opt, who had been elected by the local electoral committees in which as many as 10 percent of the voters were soon to be organized. The driving force consisted of local people with a particular interest in municipal politics, which were everywhere the source of the juiciest profits. It was they who were primarily responsible for raising the necessary funds. This newly emerging machine, which was no longer led by parliamentarians, soon found itself embroiled in conflicts with the previous power brokers and especially with the whip. Nevertheless, supported by interested local parties, the machine triumphed so convincingly that the whip was forced to accept the situation and come to terms with it. The upshot was the centralization of power in the hands of a few people, and ultimately just one person, who stood at the head of the party. For in the Liberal Party, the entire system had come into being in connection with Gladstone's rise to power. What led to such a swift victory over the notables was the fascination exerted by

---

[48] Weber used the English term.

[49] Joseph Chamberlain (1836–1914) was a leading radical politician based in Birmingham. He subsequently made a career in national politics and rose to the position of president of the Board of Trade in Gladstone's second ministry. However, having broken with the Liberals over Gladstone's policy of Home Rule for Ireland, his views gradually became increasingly imperialistic. Under the Tories he served as secretary of state for the colonies.

The notes to Weber's lecture make it clear that the parson in question is Chamberlain's long-standing collaborator, Francis Schnadhorst, who was in actual fact not a parson but a cloth merchant of nonconformist background. He became the secretary to the Birmingham Liberal Association in 1873. Later on, he was responsible for the reorganization of the party branches in other towns on the model of the Birmingham caucus.

Gladstone's "grand demagogic" skills and the masses' firm belief in the moral nature of his policies and, above all, in his personal moral qualities. A Caesarist, plebiscitary element now made its entrance on the political stage. It was the dictator of the electoral battlefield, and it quickly made itself felt. In 1877 the caucus became active for the first time in a general election, with stunning success. The result was Disraeli's fall from power in the midst of his great triumphs. By 1886 the machine had become completely identified through the power of charisma with the personality of the leader. This reached its climax at the start of the Home Rule debate,[50] when the entire apparatus from top to bottom did not ask, "Do we agree with Gladstone's policy on this question?" but simply swung behind him at his command, taking the view that "Whatever he does, we shall follow him." In so doing, the caucus simply abandoned Chamberlain, its own creator, leaving him stranded.

This machinery calls for a considerable body of people to work for it. There are probably as many as two thousand people in Britain who live directly from party politics. Far more numerous, of course, are those who are involved in politics in search of some office or other, or to serve a specific interest, especially in local government politics. For the useful caucus politician there are opportunities to gratify his vanity, in addition to the prospects for improving his economic position. In the nature of the case, to become a JP or an MP[51] is the height of (normal) ambition, and people who have had a good upbringing, and are "gentlemen," are rewarded by these titles. And in the light of the fact that perhaps as much as 50 percent of the parties' finances came in the form of gifts from anonymous donors, the greatest prize of all, particularly for wealthy benefactors, was a peerage.

What, then, has been the effect of the entire system? It is that today, with the exception of a few members of the cabinet (and a number of independently minded eccentrics), British members of Parliament have become nothing more than well-disciplined voting fodder. In Germany deputies have at least taken the trouble to deal with their private correspondence while sitting at their desks in the Reichstag and thus to act as if they were working for the good of the nation. No such gesture is required in Britain. There the member of

---

[50] Gladstone was converted to the cause of Irish Home Rule in 1885. His attempts to gain parliamentary approval for it were rejected in 1886 and again in 1893.

[51] Weber used the English initials JP and MP, as well as the term "gentlemen," here and subsequently.

Parliament has only to vote and to avoid betraying his party. He must appear when summoned by the whips and do whatever is required by the cabinet or the leader of the opposition. And as for the caucus machine outside in the country, if the leader is strong, it is almost entirely unprincipled and wholly under his control. Above Parliament, then, stands a man who is in all essentials an elected dictator who makes use of the party "machine" in order to bring the masses to heel behind him, and who regards the parliamentarians merely as political beneficiaries of the spoils system to be numbered among his followers.

Now, how does the process of selecting these leaders work? To start with: For what accomplishments are they chosen? What is crucial here, apart from the qualities of will that are decisive all over the world, is, of course, the power of demagogic speech making. The style of rhetoric has changed from what it was in Cobden's day, when it addressed itself to reason.[52] It then moved on to Gladstone, who was an expert in the seemingly sober art of "letting the facts speak for themselves," and from there it came down to the present day, when speakers frequently make use of purely emotive language of the kind also employed by the Salvation Army in order to set the masses in motion. The existing situation can properly be described as a "dictatorship based on the exploitation of the emotional nature of the masses." But the very advanced system of committee work in the British Parliament makes it possible to *take part* and also forces every politician who contemplates joining the leadership to do so. All ministers worthy of note in recent decades have undergone this very real and effective training, while the practice of reporting and criticizing the work of these committees publicly ensures that this school produces a true selection process and that it is able to eliminate the mere demagogue.

That, then, is the position in Britain. The caucus system there, however, was very diluted compared with the party organization in America, where the plebiscitary principle emerged especially early and in an especially pure form. Washington's America was supposed to be a polity administered according to his idea of a "gentleman."[53] A gentleman over there at that time was a landowner or a

---

[52] Richard Cobden (1804–65), a British politician, was one of the leading spokesmen of the free-trade movement in Britain. From 1838 he led the Anti-Corn Law League in its successful campaign to repeal the Corn Laws in 1846. The Corn Laws had sought to protect the price of grain.

[53] Weber used the English word.

man with a college education. That was indeed how America was governed initially. When parties began to form, the members of the House of Representatives at first claimed a leadership role, as in Britain at the time of the rule of the notables. Party organization was quite loose. This lasted until 1824. Even before the 1820s the party machine had started to develop in a number of local munici-palities, which here, too, were the starting point of modern develop-ments. But it was only with the election of Andrew Jackson as president, the candidate of farmers in the West, that the old tradi-tions were jettisoned. Soon after 1840 the role of congressmen in leading the parties formally came to an end when the great parlia-mentarians, like Calhoun and Webster,[54] bowed out of political life because Congress had lost almost all its power to the party machine in the country. The fact that the plebiscitary "machine" developed so early in America can be ascribed to the circumstance that there, and there alone, the head of the executive branch and hence the man in charge of official patronage—which is what counted—was a president elected by the popular will and that because of the "sepa-ration of powers" he was almost entirely independent of Congress in the conduct of his office. This meant that above all, in the case of the election of the president, genuine booty beckoned as the reward of victory and took the shape of the fruits of office. The conse-quence of this was the "spoils system,"[55] which Andrew Jackson systematically elevated into a principle.

What is the meaning for the parties nowadays of the "spoils sys-tem," that is, the allocation of all federal offices to the followers of the victorious candidate? It means that the contending parties have no principles at all; they are purely careerist organizations that change their programs for each election in accordance with what they see as their best chances of catching votes. And notwithstanding all other similarities, these programs change at a rate not to be matched elsewhere. The parties are shaped with an eye to the election campaign that is of supreme importance for the patronage of offices: the election of the president of the Union and the governorships of

---

[54] John Calhoun (1782–1850) was a leading politician who served as a congress-man, secretary of war, vice president (1825–32), and secretary of state. He was known as a champion of states' rights and became a symbol of the Old South. Daniel Webster (1782–1852) was an orator and politician. As a young lawyer, he practiced before the Supreme Court. He subsequently became a congressman, sena-tor, and secretary of state, where he made a name for himself as a defender of the Union against states' rights.

[55] Weber used the English term.

the individual states. Programs and candidates are finalized in the parties' "national conventions"[56] without the intervention of the parliamentarians. These "conventions" are party congresses that, formally, consist of representatives who have been chosen in a highly democratic manner by assemblies of delegates who, for their part, owe their own mandates to the party "primaries,"[57] the fundamental voting assemblies of the party. Even in the primaries, the delegates are selected in the name of the candidates for the supreme office of state. *Within* the individual parties bitter struggles rage for the privilege of "nomination." The fact is that between three and four hundred thousand official nominations are in the president's hands, and the task of filling them is one he undertakes himself, assisted only by the advice he receives from the senators representing the individual states. Thus the senators are powerful politicians. The House of Representatives, in contrast, is relatively impotent politically, because it lacks the authority to bestow patronage and because the ministers who are purely assistants to the president, whose rights have been legitimated by the people against everyone, including Congress, can administer their office independently of whether they enjoy its confidence or not. This, too, is a consequence of the "separation of powers."

Underpinned in this way, the spoils system was technically *possible* in America because only a youthful civilization could sustain such a purely amateurish approach to the conduct of its affairs. For it is self-evident that the existence of three to four hundred thousand party supporters who had nothing to show by way of their qualifications for office but the fact that they had served their party well— such a state of affairs could not survive without major abuses: corruption and the squandering of resources on a vast scale such as could only be borne by a nation with as yet unlimited economic prospects.

The figure who now makes his appearance together with this system of the plebiscitary party machine is the "boss." What is the boss? A political capitalist entrepreneur who procures votes at his own expense and his own risk. He may have acquired his first contacts as a lawyer or a saloon keeper or as the owner of a similar business, or perhaps as a lender. From there he casts his net still wider until he is able to "control" a certain number of votes. Once he has reached this stage, he establishes links with the neighboring bosses.

---

[56] In English in the original.

[57] Weber used the English word.

Through his energy, astuteness, and, above all, discretion, he attracts the attention of men already further advanced in their careers, and he begins to rise. The boss is indispensable to the organization of the party. It is centralized in his hands. By and large, it is he who procures the necessary funds. How does he achieve this? Well, partly through members' dues; above all, by levying a tax on the wages of the officials who have acquired their office through him and his party. And then through bribes and gratuities. Whoever wishes to circumvent one of the many laws with impunity stands in need of the boss's connivance and must pay for it. Otherwise, he has to reckon with unpleasant consequences. But even all this is not enough to provide the necessary operating capital. The boss is indispensable as the direct recipient of the donations of the great finance magnates. These magnates would not entrust sums of money for electoral purposes to any paid party official or to any person who has to make his accounts available in public. The boss with his shrewd discretion in money matters is the natural person for the capitalist circles who fund elections. The typical boss is a man of absolute sobriety. He does not strive for social standing; the "professional"[58] is looked down on in "high society." He seeks nothing but power, power as the source of money but also for its own sake. He works in the shadows; that is where he differs from the British "leader." You will not hear him speak in public; he suggests to speakers what they would be best advised to say, but he himself remains silent. He normally accepts no office for himself, except that of senator in the second chamber. For, since the constitution empowers senators to take part in the patronage of offices, the leading bosses often take up seats there in person. Offices are allocated primarily for services rendered to the party. But the allocation of posts in return for money donations is very common, and some offices have particular rates attached to them. This is a system for selling offices that would have been very familiar from the monarchies of the seventeenth and eighteenth centuries, inclusive of the papal states.

The boss has no firm political "principles"; he is completely without convictions and is interested only in how to attract votes. Not infrequently, he is a fairly uneducated man. In private, however, his life is normally correct and beyond reproach. Only in his political ethics does he inevitably adjust to the average standards of morality in political action that happen to be the norm, just as many of us Germans are likely to have done in the realm of the

---

[58] Weber used the English word.

economy when goods were in short supply and hoarding was rife.[59] The fact that as a "professional," as a professional politician, he is looked down on socially leaves him cold. The fact that he neither fills the great offices of the Union himself nor desires to do so has the advantage that where the bosses think it will attract votes, it is not uncommon for intelligent people outside the party to be adopted as candidates, well-known figures of repute and not just the old party notables, as is the case in Germany. Thus the very structure of these unprincipled parties with their socially despised power brokers has propelled able men into the presidency who would never have managed to achieve high office in Germany. Needless to say, the bosses will resist any outsider who represents a threat to their own sources of money and power. But in the competition for the goodwill of the voters, it is not unusual for them to have found themselves obliged to stoop to endorse candidates who are thought to be the enemies of corruption.

In America, then, we have party machines built on strikingly capitalist lines. They are tightly organized from top to bottom and are underpinned by stable political clubs of the type of Tammany Hall. These clubs are organized almost like religious orders and strive exclusively to maximize profits by achieving political control of town halls, above all, since these are the most desirable objects of exploitation. What made this structure of party life possible was the high degree of democratization of the United States because it was "a young country." This connection between youth and democracy means that now, however, the system is in slow decline. America cannot continue to be ruled by amateurs. Fifteen years ago, when one asked American workers why they let themselves be governed by politicians whom they professed to despise, they would answer: "We would rather our officials were people we spit on, than be like you and be ruled by a caste of officials who spit on us." That was the old attitude of American "democracy." Yet even at that time the socialists took a completely different view, and this situation is no longer tolerated. Government by amateurs no longer suffices, and the Civil Service Reform[60] is now creating lifelong pensionable posts in constantly growing numbers. In consequence, posts are now being filled by university-educated officials who are just as incorruptible and

---

[59] When food was in short supply during the war, as a consequence of the Allied blockade of Germany, it became customary to make excursions to the countryside, where the farmers still had food supplies that they were willing to sell.

[60] This phrase is in English.

competent as in Germany. Around one hundred thousand offices are no longer objects for booty after each election but are pensionable and dependent upon a candidate's qualifications. This will gradually push the spoils system into the background, and the face of the party leadership will probably change then, as well. The only thing is that we do not yet know in what way.

In *Germany,* the crucial factors influencing the operation of politics have been essentially as follows. First, the impotence of the parliaments. The consequence was that no one with leadership qualities wished to stay in Parliament for the longer term. Suppose anyone did wish to enter Parliament—what could he achieve there? If a post fell vacant in a chancellory he could say to the departmental head concerned: "I have a very competent man in my constituency. He would be a suitable candidate. Why don't you take him?" And this was readily agreed. But that was more or less all that a German member of Parliament could do to satisfy his instincts for power—if he had any. In addition, and this second factor was what underlay the first, there was the enormous importance of the trained, professional civil service in Germany. In this respect we in Germany led the world. The professional civil service was so important that it was able to assert its claims not just to civil service posts but also to ministerial office. Only last year someone remarked during the debate on "parliamentarization" in the Bavarian Provincial Diet that talented people would refuse to become officials if ministerial posts were given to members of Parliament. Officialdom proved able to evade systematically the kind of control exerted in Britain by debates in committee. In this way the German parliaments were prevented (with very few exceptions) from producing really competent administrative heads from among their numbers.

The third factor was that Germany, in contrast to America, had parties based on political conviction that claimed, at least ostensibly in good faith, that their members represented particular "worldviews." However, the two most important of these parties, the Center Party and the Social Democratic Party, were born minority parties, and this was in accordance with their declared intentions.[61] The leading circles of the Center Party never disguised the fact that they were opposed to parliamentary rule, because they feared that this would condemn them to be in the minority and that this in turn

---

[61] The Center Party was destined to remain a minority party because it essentially represented Roman Catholics in Germany; the same thing is true of Social Democracy, which set out to represent only the working class.

would make it harder than before to find posts for their careerists, as they had done previously, by exerting pressure on the government. Social Democracy was a minority party on principle and an obstacle to the introduction of parliamentary government because it did not wish to become contaminated by contact with the existing bourgeois political order. The fact that both parties excluded themselves from the parliamentary system made that system unworkable.

What, then, was the fate of professional politicians in Germany? They had no power or responsibility and could only play a somewhat inferior role as notables. The consequence was that they were animated once again by the typical instincts to be found in "guilds" everywhere. In the circle of these notables who made their living from whatever little positions they held, it was impossible for men not cast in the same mold to rise to prominence. I could list a large number of names from every party, and, of course, that includes Social Democracy, of people whose political careers ended in tragedy because they involved men who had leadership qualities but who were not tolerated by the notables for that very reason. All our parties have experienced this development into a guild of notables. Bebel,[62] for example, was still a leader by virtue of his temperament and integrity, however modest his intellectual accomplishments were. The fact that he was a martyr, that he never abused the trust of the masses (in their eyes, at least), meant that they stood behind him to a man, and there was no power in the party that could have provided him with a serious challenge. After his death this situation came to an end, and the rule of the officials began. Trade union officials, party secretaries, and journalists all came to the fore; bureaucratic instincts dominated the party, a highly principled bureaucracy—of rare integrity, we may say, when we consider conditions in other countries, particularly the frequently corrupt union officials in America—but the consequences of bureaucracy already alluded to also made their appearance in the party.

From the 1880s onward, the bourgeois parties became guilds of notables pure and simple. It is true that occasionally the parties attracted able minds from outside the party for publicity purposes and so that they could say, "we have this or that famous person in our ranks." As far as possible, however, they made sure that these

---

[62] August Bebel (1840–1913) was one of the cofounders of the Social Democratic Party in Germany. He was elected to the Reichstag in 1875 and led the party until his death. Weber refers to him as a martyr because under Bismarck's anti-Socialist legislation, Bebel was repeatedly imprisoned for his convictions.

people did not stand for election, and only where it was unavoidable and one or other of them insisted did it occur.

The same spirit prevails in Parliament. Our parliamentary parties were guilds and still are. Every speech that is made in the plenary sessions of the Reichstag is previously subjected to a thoroughgoing censorship in the party. This explains why they are so unutterably boring. The only members who can speak are those who have been summoned. A more glaring contrast with the British practice, or indeed the French system (though for entirely opposite reasons), is scarcely imaginable.

At present, following the gigantic upheaval that people customarily refer to as a revolution, a change may now be in progress. Perhaps, but it is not certain. The change began when we started to observe new kinds of party organization. These were amateur organizations in the first instance. They were staffed frequently by students from the different universities who would say to a man to whom they ascribed leadership qualities, "We shall do what has to be done for you, if you tell us what it is." Second, there were commercial organizations. People would come to men to whom they ascribed leadership qualities and offer to take over the business of canvassing for votes in exchange for a fixed payment for each vote. If you were to ask me which of the two methods I would regard as the more reliable from a technical and political point of view, I would, I believe, prefer the second. But both were bubbles that quickly appeared and vanished again just as quickly. The existing apparatuses reorganized themselves but kept on functioning. Such phenomena were merely symptomatic of the belief that new apparatuses would automatically appear if only there were leaders. But the technical characteristics of proportional representation were sufficient to preclude their emergence in advance. Only a few dictators of the street made their appearance, and they then disappeared once more.[63] And only the dictatorship of the street has a following that is subject to an order of strict discipline. It is this that explains the power of these tiny minorities.

If we assume that this were to change, we need to be clear, after what we have already said, that to put plebiscitary leaders in charge of parties means that their followers suffer from a "loss of soul," what we might call their spiritual proletarianization. To be of use as

---

[63] Weber's marginal note makes it clear that he was thinking of the establishment of the German Communist Party by Karl Liebknecht and Rosa Luxemburg in December 1918. They were murdered by right-wing extremists on January 15, 1919.

an apparatus for their leader they must obey blindly, they must become a machine in the American sense, undisturbed by the vanity of notables or by any pretentions to opinions of their own. Lincoln's election was made possible only by an organization of this type, and as we have pointed out, the caucus had the same function in Gladstone's case. That is the price that has to be paid for having leaders. But there is only this stark choice: either a democracy with a leader together with a "machine" or a leaderless democracy, in other words, the rule of the "professional politicians" who have no vocation and who lack the inner, charismatic qualities that turn a man into a leader. And that leads to what the rebels in any given party usually call rule by a "clique." For the time being we have only the latter in Germany. And for the future, this situation will be guaranteed, for the Reich at least, first, by the likelihood that the Upper House [*Bundesrat*] will be revived, which will necessarily restrict the power of the Reichstag and with that its importance as a place from which leaders are selected. It will be guaranteed, second, by the system of proportional representation as it exists at present. This is a typical feature of a leaderless democracy, not only because it favors horse-trading among the notables for positions but also because it opens the doors for pressure groups to force the inclusion of their officials in the lists, thus creating an unpolitical parliament in which there is no room for genuine leaders.

The only safety valve for the desire for leadership could be provided by the office of president of the Reich if the president were to be directly elected, instead of indirectly, by Parliament. Leaders could emerge and be selected on the basis of proven ability if, in the large municipalities, directly elected town dictators were to make their appearance on the scene with the right to provide their own administrative personnel. This is what happened in the United States, wherever a serious attempt was made to combat corruption. But this could come about only if a party organization existed that was tailored to the needs of such elections. But because all petty bourgeois parties are hostile to leaders, including and above all Social Democracy, we cannot say anything about the future shape the parties will take and what prospects there are of such ideas becoming a reality.

It is not possible to see today, therefore, how the business of politics can take the outward shape of a "profession," and even less what prospects of a worthwhile political challenge might open up for people who are politically talented. The man who is compelled by his financial situation to live "from" politics will always find that the typical direct paths will involve choosing between journalism or a post as party official. Or else he could consider a post with one of the representative bodies: trade union, chamber of commerce, farmers' association, craft workers' chamber, industrial chamber, employers' associations, and so on, or the appropriate positions in local government. Nothing further can be said about the outward shape of the profession except that the party official shares with the journalist the odium of being "*déclassé.*" He will, unfortunately, always have the actual or unspoken rebuke of "hired hack" ringing in his ears, in the case of the journalist, or "hired speaker," in the case of the official. Anyone who lacks inner defenses against accusations of this kind and is unable to find the proper retort to them should avoid such a career, because in addition to the risk of exposing himself to grave temptations, he may find that it turns out to be full of disappointments.

We may inquire what inner pleasures may be expected from a political career and what are the personal qualifications called for in those who choose it?

Well, to start with, it provides a sense of power. Even in what may be quite a modest post formally, the professional politician may feel he has been raised above the commonplace by his discovery that he has influence on people, that he has his share of power over them, but above all that he holds in his hands a strand of some important historical process. But the question now confronting such a politician is: What qualities does he need to do justice to this power (however narrowly circumscribed it may be) and hence to the responsibility that it imposes on him? This takes us onto the terrain of ethical questions. For to ask what kind of a human being one must be to have the right to grasp the spokes of the wheel of history is to ask an ethical question.

We can say that three qualities, above all, are of decisive importance for a politician: passion, a sense of responsibility, and a sense of proportion. Passion in the sense of a *commitment to the matter in hand* [*Sachlichkeit*], that is, the passionate dedication to a "cause" [*Sache*], to the God or demon that presides over it. Not in the sense of that inner state of mind that my late friend Georg Simmel was in the habit of describing as "sterile excitement." That state of mind is characteristic of a certain type of intellectual, Russian intellectuals above all (though by no means all of them!), and now plays such a great part among our intellectuals, too, in this carnival that is being flattered with the proud name of "revolution." For this excitement is no more than an aimless and unfocused "romanticism of the intellectually interesting," devoid of a sense of responsibility for any cause whatever. For mere passion, however sincerely felt, is not enough in itself. It cannot make a politician of anyone, unless service to a "cause" also means that a sense of *responsibility* toward that cause is made the decisive guiding light of action. And for that (and this is the crucial psychological characteristic of the politician) *a sense of proportion* is required, the ability to allow realities to impinge on you while maintaining an inner calm and composure. What is needed, in short, is a *distance* from people and things. The "absence of distance," pure and simple, is one of the deadly sins of every politician and one of those qualities which, if instilled into our intellectuals, will condemn them to political impotence. For the heart of the problem is how to forge a unity between hot passion and a cool sense of proportion in one and the same person. Politics is made with the mind, not with other parts of the body or the soul. And yet if politics is to be an authentic human activity and not just a frivolous intellectual game, commitment to it must be born of passion and be nourished by it. Even so, the ability to keep the soul in check is what characterizes the passionate politician and distinguishes his attitude from the "sterile excitement" of the amateur. This can be achieved only by acquiring the habit of distance, in every sense of the word. The "strength" of a political "personality" means, primarily, the possession of these qualities.

Thus the politician is faced daily and hourly with the task of overcoming in himself a very trivial, all-too-human enemy: common or garden *vanity*, the deadly enemy of all dedication to a cause and of all distance, in this case, the distance from oneself.

Vanity is a very widespread quality, and perhaps no one is entirely free of it. And in academic and scholarly circles it is a kind of occupational disease. But in the case of the scholar, repugnant though it may be, it is relatively innocuous in the sense that as a rule it does not disrupt the business of scholarship. It is quite otherwise with politicians. For politicians, the striving for *power* is an unavoidable tool [*Mittel*] of their trade. Thus the "power instinct," as it is often called, belongs among their normal attributes. However, the sin against the Holy Spirit of their profession begins where this striving for power is *separated from the matter in hand* and becomes an object purely of self-intoxication instead of something that enters exclusively into the service of their "cause." For ultimately there are only two kinds of mortal sin in the field of politics: the lack of commitment to a cause and the lack of a sense of responsibility that is often, but not always, identical with it. Vanity, the need to thrust oneself center stage, is what is most likely to lead the politician into the temptation of committing either or both of these sins. All the more, as the demagogue is forced to play for "effect." Because he is concerned only with the "impression" he is making, he always runs the risk both of turning into an actor and of taking too lightly his responsibility for his own actions. His lack of objectivity leads him to strive for the glittering facade of power, instead of its reality, while his lack of a sense of responsibility seduces him into enjoying power for its own sake, rather than for its substantive purpose. For although, or rather *because,* power is an unavoidable tool of all politics, and the striving for power, therefore, is one of its driving forces, there is no more destructive distortion of political energy than when the parvenu swaggers around, boasting of his power, conceitedly reveling in its reflected glory—or indeed any worship of power for its own sake. An energetically fostered cult that has grown up in Germany, as elsewhere, has sought to idealize the mere "power politician." Such figures may make a strong impression, but in actual fact their activity is empty and meaningless. The critics of "power politics" are completely right about this. There have been a number of instances when the typical representatives of this cast of mind have suddenly suffered an inner collapse, exposing the internal weakness and impotence lurking behind this showy but entirely vacuous pose. This pose is the product of an exceedingly impoverished and superficial indifference toward the *meaning* of human activity, a blasé attitude that remains completely blind to the tragedy in which all action is ensnared, political action above all.

It is entirely true and a fundamental fact of all history (though one we cannot explore further here) that the ultimate product of political activity frequently, indeed, as a matter of course, fails utterly to do justice to its original purpose and may even be a travesty of it. Nevertheless, this purpose, this service on behalf of a *cause,* cannot be dispensed with if action is to have any internal support. The *nature* of the cause in whose service the politician strives for power and makes use of power is a matter of belief. He may serve national or universally human goals, social and ethical goals, or goals that are cultural, worldly, or religious. He may be motivated by a powerful faith in "progress" (however this is defined), or he may coolly reject faith of this kind; he can claim to be acting in the service of an "idea," or he may wish to reject such claims on principle and choose instead to promote external goals of ordinary life. But some belief or other must always be *present.* Otherwise, even what seem outwardly to be the most glorious political successes will be cursed—and rightly so—because they will have no more meaning and purpose than events in the animal kingdom.

What we have said up to now has brought us to a discussion of the final problem that preoccupies us this evening: the *ethos* of politics as a "cause." Quite apart from its specific goals, what vocation can politics have within the overall moral economy of our conduct of life? Where is what we might term the ethical location in which politics is at home? At this point we find ourselves caught up in a conflict of ultimate worldviews, and it falls to us to *choose* between them. Let us then make a resolute attempt to tackle this problem, which has recently been addressed from what is in my view a completely wrong angle.

Let us begin by liberating it from a quite trivial distortion. Ethics can sometimes make its appearance in what is morally a highly unfortunate role. Let us consider some examples. Take the case of a man whose affections have turned away from one woman to another. He will be an unusual man if he does not experience the need to justify this to himself by saying, "She was not worthy of my love" or "She has disappointed me" or by coming up with other "reasons" of a similar sort. This is a highly unchivalrous reaction to the blunt reality that he no longer loves her and that she must put up with that. Even more unchivalrously, he goes on to invent a "legitimacy" that enables him to put himself in the right and add to her misfortune by trying to put her in the wrong. The successful rival for a woman's affections behaves in like manner: his predecessor must be the more worthless of the two, for he would not otherwise have emerged the loser. And obviously, it is no different after a victorious war when the victor asserts with a wholly discreditable self-righteousness, "I won because I was in the right." Or, take the case of a man who collapses mentally under the strain of the horrors of war. Instead simply of saying, "It was all too much," he may feel the need to justify his own war weariness to himself by replacing it with the feeling that he could not put up with any more because he had been forced to fight for an immoral cause. And the same thing holds true for those on the losing side. There is no point in complaining like old women who start looking for the "guilty party" once the war is over, when in reality the war was the product of the structures of society. Instead, every uncomplaining, manly person will say to the enemy: "We lost the war—you have won it. That's over and done with. So let us now talk about what conclusions we must draw with regard to the *objective* [*sachlichen*] interests that were at stake, and—this is the main thing—in the light of our responsibility for the *future,* which must weigh most heavily on the victor." Everything else is unworthy and will exact its own retribution. A nation can forgive damage to its interests, but not an assault on its honor, least of all in the spirit of sanctimonious self-righteousness. Every new document that comes to light after decades have passed will revive undignified quarrels and stir up all the hatred and anger once more, whereas our task should be to make sure that *morally* the war is laid to rest once it is over. This can be achieved only through a combination of matter-of-factness and chivalry and, above all, by respecting other people's *dignity.* It can never be brought about by an "ethic" that amounts in reality to undignified behavior on both sides. Instead of focusing on those issues that concern the politician, namely, the future and our responsibility for the future, such an ethic becomes immersed in questions of past guilt, which are politically sterile because they can never be resolved. To become *so immersed* is political guilt if anything is. In the process, moreover, the participants can easily overlook the inevitable distortion of the entire problem by very material interests: the interest of the victor in securing the greatest possible gains, both moral and material, the hopes of the defeated that they will obtain various concessions in exchange for confessions of guilt.[64] If anything is truly *mean and base,* this is it, and it is the consequence of using "ethics" to "prove" one is "in the right."

If that is so, what is the true relation between ethics and politics? Have they absolutely nothing in common, as has occasionally been maintained? Or is the opposite the case: that the ethic that applies to political action is "the same ethic" that holds true for any other activity? It has sometimes been claimed that these two assertions are mutually exclusive. Either one or the other must be right. But is it then true that there is any system of ethics in the world in which substantially the *same* commandments can be proposed for all relationships, whether erotic, business, family and official relations, relations to one's wife, the greengrocer's assistant, one's son, competitors, friends, and the accused in the dock? Can the ethical demands made

---

[64] Weber alludes here to the policy adopted by Kurt Eisner, who was briefly prime minister in Bavaria. Eisner, together with large parts of his own party, the Independent Socialists (USPD), was convinced that Germany's position in the peace negotiations would be improved by the unreserved confession of Germany's guilt for the outbreak of World War I. Accordingly, he published documents showing that the German government had encouraged Austria-Hungary to take a hard line toward Serbia and had consciously accepted the risk of widening the conflict to embrace the whole of Europe. See the Introduction.

on politics really be quite indifferent to the fact that politics operates with a highly specific means, namely, power, behind which *violence* lies concealed? Is it not obvious that the Bolshevist and Spartacist[65] ideologues are achieving exactly the *same* results as any militarist dictator precisely because they use this tool of politics? How, then, other than by the identity of the rulers and their amateurish ways, are we to distinguish the rule of the Councils of Workers and Soldiers[66] from that of any potentate under the old regime? How are we to distinguish between the polemics leveled by the majority of the representatives of the supposedly new ethics at the opponents they criticize and the polemics of any other demagogues? By their noble intentions, we shall be told! Well and good. But it is the methods they use that we are talking about here, and the nobility of their ultimate intentions is also claimed by the people they oppose and with a sincerity that is just as genuine. "All they that take the sword shall perish with the sword,"[67] and conflict is everywhere the same. So, what about the ethics of the *Sermon on the Mount*? The Sermon on the Mount (and by this is meant the absolute ethics of the Gospel) is a far more serious business than is imagined by those who like to quote its commandments nowadays. In truth, it is no laughing matter. We may say of it what has been said about causality in science: it is no hansom cab that can be stopped anywhere, to jump into or out of at will.[68] Rather, the sermon is a matter of all *or* nothing; *that* is the point of it

---

[65] The Spartakus League (named in memory of a slave who had led a rebellion in ancient Rome) was a left-wing socialist group that was established in 1916 in opposition to World War I. In December 1918 it re-formed itself into the German Communist Party (KPD).

[66] These revolutionary councils (= "soviets") were established in Russia after the February Revolution of 1917. Nominally, they were the chief organ of revolutionary authority, but in practice their powers were undermined by the growing ascendancy of the centralizing Communist Party. In Germany, similar councils were set up in November 1918, and they forced the kaiser and the other German princes into abdication and exile. After attempts to seize power regionally (e.g., in Bavaria) and nationally, they were defeated in the spring of 1919 and put down brutally by an alliance of troops belonging to the central government and the so-called *Freikorps,* militias made up of extreme right-wing volunteers who had been demobilized from the regular army after the defeat of Germany.

[67] Matthew 26:52.

[68] The metaphor is derived from Arthur Schopenhauer, who asserted that the "Law of causality is not so obliging as to let itself be used like a cab, to be dismissed when we have reached our destination." See "The Fourfold Root of the Principle of Sufficient Reason," in Julius Frauenstädt, ed., *Sämmtliche Werke*, vol. 1 (Leipzig: Brockhaus, 1898), p. 38.

if it is to amount to anything more than a set of platitudes. For example, consider the rich young man who "went away sorrowful: for he was one that had great possessions."[69] The Gospel's commandment is unconditional and unambiguous: give up everything that thou hast—absolutely *everything*. The politician will say that socially this is a senseless demand as long as it does not apply to *everyone*. That means taxation, redistribution, confiscation—in a word, coercion and order applied to *everyone*. The ethical commandment, however, ignores such matters *entirely; that* is its nature. Or again, consider the commandment to "turn the other cheek." Unconditionally, without asking why the other person has lashed out at you. An ethic of ignominy [*Würdelosigkeit*]—except for a saint. That is the crux of the matter: you must be a saint in *all* respects or at least want to be one; you must live like Jesus, the apostles, St. Francis, and their like, and *then* this ethic will make sense and be the expression of true dignity. But *not otherwise*. For if, following this unworldly ethic of love, you ought to "resist not him that is evil with violence"[70]—the politician must abide by the opposite commandment: "You *shall* use force to resist evil, for otherwise you will be *responsible* for its running amok." Anyone who wishes to act in accordance with the ethic of the Gospel should abstain from going on strike—for strikes are a form of coercion. Instead, he should join the company unions. Above all, such a person should not speak of "revolution." For surely this ethic does not intend to teach that of all wars civil war is the only legitimate one. The pacifist who acts in accordance with the Gospel will refuse to take up arms or will throw them away, as was recommended in Germany, so that we might perform our moral duty to put an end to the war and thus to all war. The politician will say that the only certain way to discredit war for the *foreseeable* future would have been a peace on the basis of the *status quo*. For in that event the nations would have asked themselves why the war had been fought. It would have been fought for nothing at all, an absurdity. But that is now not possible. For the war will have turned out to be politically profitable for the victors, or at least for some of them. And what is responsible for that result is the very behavior that made it impossible for us to resist in the first place. Now, once the period of exhaustion is over, *it is peace that will be discredited, not war*. And this will be the consequence of an absolutist ethic.

---

[69] Matthew 19:21.

[70] "But I say unto you, Resist not him that is evil: but whosoever smiteth thee on thy right cheek, turn to him the other also" (Matthew 5:39).

Finally, there is the duty to tell the truth. For an absolutist ethic this duty is paramount. Some people have inferred from this, therefore, that what was needed was the publication of all documents, especially those that incriminated our own nation. And what followed from this unilateral publication was a confession of guilt, itself one-sided, unconditional and heedless of its consequences. The politician will find that the cause of truth is not advanced by the misuse of these documents and the renewed unleashing of passions but rather is certain to be obscured by it. He will discover that only an all-around systematic inquiry by nonpartisan witnesses could be fruitful, while every other approach may well lead to consequences for the nation that cannot be made good for decades. But an absolutist ethic simply refuses to *inquire* about "consequences."

This is the crucial point. We need to be clear that all ethically oriented action can be guided by either of two fundamentally different, irredeemably incompatible maxims: it can be guided by an "ethics of conviction" or an "ethics of responsibility." This does not mean that an ethics of conviction is identical with irresponsibility or an ethics of responsibility with a lack of conviction. Needless to say, there can be no question of that. But there is a profound abyss between acting in accordance with the maxim governing an ethics of conviction and acting in tune with an ethics of responsibility. In the former case this means, to put it in religious terms: "A Christian does what is right and leaves the outcome to God,"[71] while in the latter you must answer for the (foreseeable) *consequences* of your actions. You may be able to prove to a syndicalist[72] who is a convinced adherent of an ethics of conviction that in all likelihood the consequences of his actions will be to improve the prospects of the reactionaries, to increase the oppression of his own class and to hamper its rise. But however convincing your proofs may be, you

---

[71] According to the editors of the *Gesamtausgabe* of Max Weber's writings, this quotation may be traced back to a remark made by Luther in his lecture on the book of Genesis, "Fac tuum officium, et eventum Deo permitte," D. *Martin Luthers Werke, Kritische Gesamtausgabe,* vol. 44 (Weimar: Böhlhaus-Nachfolger, 1915), p. 78.

[72] Syndicalism wished to bring about the emancipation of the working class by means of "direct action" against the immediate class enemy—that is, the employers. Direct action included general strikes as demonstrations but not parliamentary methods as traditional trade-union tactics. Although such action was not expected to lead immediately to the overthrow of capitalism, it was hoped that in time the foundations of capitalism would be shaken. Syndicalism's ultimate goal was a decentralized society based on self-managing production units, not the all-embracing bureaucratic system aspired to by Socialist parties.

will make no impression on him at all. Such a man believes that if an action performed out of pure conviction has evil consequences, then the responsibility must lie not with the agent but with the world, the stupidity of men—or the will of God who created them thus. With the ethics of responsibility, on the other hand, a man reckons with exactly those average human failings. As Fichte has justly pointed out, he has absolutely no right to assume human-kind's goodness and perfection.[73] He does not feel that he is in a position to shift the consequences of his actions, where they are foreseeable, onto others. He will say, "These consequences are to be ascribed to my actions." With an ethics of conviction, one feels "responsible" only for ensuring that the flame of pure conviction, for example, the flame of protest against the injustice of the social order, should never be extinguished. To keep on reigniting it is the purpose of his actions. These actions, when judged from the stand-point of their possible success, are entirely irrational; they can and should have merely exemplary value.

But even this does not exhaust the problem. No ethic in the world can ignore the fact that in many cases the achievement of "good" ends is inseparable from the use of morally dubious or at least dan-gerous means and that we cannot escape the possibility or even probability of evil side effects. And no ethic in the world can say when, and to what extent, the ethically good end can "justify" the ethically dangerous means and its side effects.

In politics, the decisive means is the use of force. The extent of the moral tension between means and ends can be gauged from the case of the revolutionary Socialists (of the Zimmerwald tendency).[74] As is

---

[73] Fichte cites a passage from Machiavelli's *The Discourses* in which the latter advises every statesman to act on the assumption that humankind's evil nature is a basic fact of life, and that people instantly display this evil nature whenever the opportunity arises. Fichte adds that this fundamental principle of Machiavelli's political doctrine is self-evidently true and has lost none of its validity. *Johann Gott-lieb Fichtes Nachgelassene Werke*, vol. 3 (Bonn: A. Marcus, 1835), p. 420.

[74] The Zimmerwald tendency refers to a conference of Socialists held in Zimmer-wald in Switzerland in September 1915 to work out an "internationalist" response to the war and counter the national loyalties to which Socialists of the belligerent nations had fallen prey. It was attended most notably by Lenin, although his radical point of view did not prevail. He had called for an appeal to soldiers and workers to lay down their arms and go on strike against the war. However, French Socialists pointed out that Lenin would be quite safe in Switzerland, while any soldiers and workers following his advice would be liable to the death penalty for treason. The compromise manifesto adopted called for "peace without indemnities and without annexations" on the basis of the "self-determination of peoples."

generally known, even during the war these Socialists adopted the principle that we might succinctly formulate as follows: "If we face the choice of either another few years' war, after which there will be revolution, or else peace now but no revolution, our choice must be: another few years' war!" And to the further question: "What can this revolution achieve?" every scientifically schooled Socialist would have answered that there could be no question of a transition to an economy that could be called Socialist in *his* sense of the word. Instead, yet another bourgeois economy would emerge, but with the difference that its feudal elements and the vestiges of dynastic rule would have been stripped away. So they would approve of "another few years' war"—for this modest gain! We shall surely be permitted to say that however firm our Socialist convictions might be, we might legitimately reject the end that called for such means. But this is precisely the situation with Bolshevism and Spartacism and indeed with revolutionary socialism of every kind. It is, of course, ludicrous to see the Socialists *morally* denouncing the "politicians of violence" of the old regime for making use of exactly the same means as they are willing to use themselves—however justified they may be in rejecting their *ends*.

Here, with this problem of justifying the means by the ends, we see the inevitable failure of an ethics of conviction in general. And in fact, it logically has only one possibility. That is to *repudiate every* action that makes use of morally suspect means, logically. In the world of realities, of course, we see again and again how the representatives of an ethics of conviction suddenly become transformed into chiliastic[75] prophets. For example, people who have just preached "love against force" are found calling for the use of force the very next moment. It is always the very *last* use of force that will then bring about a situation in which *all* violence will have been destroyed—just as our military leaders tell the soldiers that every offensive will be the last. This one will bring victory and then peace. The man who embraces an ethics of conviction is unable to tolerate the ethical irrationality of the world. He is a cosmic, ethical "rationalist." All of you who know your Dostoyevsky will remember the scene with the Grand Inquisitor,[76] where the problem is

---

[75] That is, prophets who believe in a future thousand-year age of blessedness, the Second Coming of Christ or a Golden Age.

[76] From Dostoyevsky's *The Brothers Karamazov,* book 5, chapter 5. In that scene Christ reappears in Seville at the time of the Inquisition, only to be re-arrested and sentenced to death by the Grand Inquisitor because his presence interferes with the power of the church, which alone understands how to distribute bread among humankind and to save them from the curse of freedom.

cogently set out. It is not possible to reconcile an ethics of conviction with an ethics of responsibility or to decree which end can justify *which* means, if indeed you wish to make any concessions to this principle at all.

My colleague F. W. Foerster,[77] whom I esteem very highly personally because of the undoubted integrity of his convictions, while rejecting him unconditionally as a politician, expresses the belief in his book that we can get around the difficulty with the aid of the simple thesis that nothing but good can come from good and nothing but evil from evil. Needless to say, if that were true, the entire problem would cease to exist. But it is astonishing for such an assertion to see the light of day 2,500 years after the first appearance of the Upanishads. Not only the entire course of world history but also every dispassionate scrutiny of our everyday experience tells us the opposite. The history of every religion on earth is based on the conviction that the reverse is true. After all, the age-old problem of theodicy asks the question: How could a power that is said to be both omnipotent and good create such an irrational world of unmerited suffering, unpunished injustice, and incorrigible stupidity? Either that power is not omnipotent or it is not good, or else—a third possibility—life is governed by completely different principles of compensation and retribution, principles that we can interpret metaphysically or that are destined always to elude our attempts at interpretation. This problem, the experience of the irrationality of the universe, has always been the driving force of the entire history of religion. The Indian doctrine of *karma,* Persian dualism, original sin, predestination, and the *deus absconditus*[78] have all grown out of this experience. The early Christians, too, were well aware that the world was governed by demons and that whoever becomes involved with politics, that is to say, with power and violence as a means, has made a pact with satanic powers. It follows that as far as a person's actions are concerned, it is *not* true that nothing but good comes from good and nothing but evil from evil, but rather quite frequently the opposite is the case. Anyone who does not realize this is in fact a mere child in political matters.

---

[77] See note 19 in "Science as a Vocation." The book referred to here is his *Staatsbürgerliche Erziehung* (Leipzig and Berlin: Teubner, 1914), p. 202.

[78] The idea that God is hidden, that is, that revelation cannot be fully communicated in books and sermons, is found in many religions, including Hasidic Judaism and the Hinduism of the Upanishads. A strain of Christian theology has argued that God is best known through a "negative" theology that makes no positive statements about God. This idea was taken up by, among others, Martin Luther, who maintained that the revealed God remained the *hidden God.*

Religious ethics has made various accommodations with the fact that we find ourselves placed in different cultures [*Lebensordnungen*], each of which is subject to different laws. The Hellenistic polytheism sacrificed to Aphrodite as well as to Hera, to Dionysos as well as to Apollo, knowing full well that these divinities were often at loggerheads with one another. The Hindu culture made each of the different professions into the object of a particular ethical law, a *dharma*. It then placed them in castes, separating them from one another forever in a fixed hierarchy from which there was no escape for those born into a particular caste, other than through their reincarnation in the next life. In this way the different occupations were positioned at varying distances from the highest spiritual goods. This made it possible for Hinduism to elaborate the *dharma* of each individual caste in accordance with the intrinsic laws governing each profession, from the ascetics and the Brahmans down to the villains and whores. These included war and politics. One can see how war was inserted into the general culture in the *Bhagavad Gita,* in the dialogue between Krishna and Arjuna. "Do what is necessary," in other words, do whatever "work" is prescribed by the *dharma* of the warrior caste and its rules as a duty necessary for the conduct of war. According to this faith, to do this "work" does not detract from religious salvation but contributes to it.[79] Acceptance into Indra's heaven[80] was as certain a reward for the Indian warrior who had died a hero's death as was Valhalla for the Germanic warrior. But the Indian warrior would have scorned nirvana just as his Germanic equivalent would have despised the Christian paradise with its angelic choirs. This specialized approach to ethics made it possible for Indian philosophy to develop an internally consistent treatment of the royal art of politics, focusing entirely on its own particular laws and indeed intensifying them radically. A genuinely radical "Machiavellianism," in the popular sense of the word,

---

[79] The *Bhagavad Gita,* or "Song of God," which was written in the first or second century AD, is regarded as one of the greatest of the Hindu scriptures. It consists of a dialogue between Prince Arjuna and his friend and charioteer Krishna, who is also an earthly incarnation of the god Vishnu. The discussion takes place on the eve of battle, when Arjuna sees many of his kinsmen and friends lined up on the opposing side. He considers whether it would not be better to throw down his arms and allow himself to be slain than to engage in a just but cruel war. Krishna recalls him to his sense of duty as a warrior by pointing out to him that the higher way is the dispassionate discharge of his duty, performed with faith in God and without selfish concern for personal triumph or gain.

[80] Indra was the warrior king of the heavens, the god of war and storm.

received its classic formulation in Indian literature as early as Kautilya's *Arthashastra*[81] (long before the Christian era, allegedly from the time of Chandragupta). Machiavelli's *The Prince* is harmless in comparison. It is well known that in Catholic ethics, which Foerster generally finds congenial, the *consilia evangelica*[82] constitute a special ethics intended for those endowed with the charisma of the holy life. In it we find the monk who may not shed blood or earn his living, and next to him the pious knight and the burgher, of whom the one may do the first and the other the second. The hierarchy of ethical goods and its integration in an organic doctrine of salvation is less logical than in India, as was only to be expected, given the premises of the Christian faith. The corruption of the world through original sin should have made it relatively simple to integrate violence into ethics as a way of punishing sin and the heretics who placed human souls in jeopardy.

However, the unworldly imperatives of the Sermon on the Mount, which are in complete harmony with an ethics of conviction, and the absolute demands made by the religious natural law based on it retained their revolutionary power. In almost every age of social upheaval they appeared on the scene with elemental force. In particular they created the radical, pacifist sects, one of which, in Pennsylvania, tried the experiment of a polity that refused to use force in its relations with the outside world. This proved tragic in the event since, when the War of Independence broke out, the Quakers were unable to take up arms in defense of their ideals, even though it was those ideals that were being defended in the war.

Normal Protestantism, in contrast, legitimated the state, in other words, the use of force, absolutely, as a divine institution, and in particular it endorsed the legitimate authoritarian state. Luther absolved the individual from the ethical responsibility for war and shifted that burden onto the shoulders of the authorities. To obey them in matters not affecting faith, it was held, could never be wrong. In the same way Calvinism accepted the use of force in principle as a means of defending the faith, religious war, in short. This had been Islam's natural element from the very outset. It is evident

---

[81] Kautilya was an Indian statesman and philosopher who was said to have been the chief minister and adviser to King Chandragupta (c. 300 BC), the founder of the Maurya dynasty. His work, the *Arthashastra* (The Handbook of [the King's] Profit) was regarded as a foundational text on the state. It appeared originally in 321–296 BC. The third English edition appeared in 1929.

[82] The *consilia evangelica* are a body of instructions for living a Christian life; they emphasize celibacy, poverty, and obedience.

that the problem of political ethics is *not* simply the product of the modern rejection of faith that springs from the cult of the hero during the Renaissance. All religions have wrestled with it, with widely differing success; and what we have said makes it clear that things could not be otherwise. The specific use of *legitimate force* purely as such in the hands of human organizations is what determines the particular nature of all ethical problems in politics.

Whoever makes a pact with the use of force, for whatever ends (and every politician does so), is at the mercy of its particular consequences. The man who fights for his faith, whether religious or revolutionary, is particularly exposed to this risk. We need not look beyond the present to find examples. Anyone who desires to use *force* to establish absolute justice on earth needs followers, a human "apparatus." He must be able to hold out the prospect of the necessary internal and external prizes (heavenly and earthly rewards), or else this apparatus will not function. Given the conditions of modern class conflict, what is meant by internal reward is the gratification of hatred and the desire for vengeance, and especially of resentment and the need for a pseudoethical feeling of self-righteousness, in other words, the felt need to slander your opponents and denounce them as heretics. By external prizes we mean adventure, victory, booty, power, and the rewards of office. The leader is entirely dependent for his success on the functioning of this apparatus. He is dependent, therefore, on *its* motives, not on his own. He is therefore dependent on being able to keep providing the followers he relies on—the Red Guard,[83] the informers, the agitators—with these rewards *in perpetuity.* Since his activities must be carried out under these conditions, it is evident that what he in fact achieves is not in his own hands but is laid down for him by the predominantly base motives governing the actions of his followers. For they can only be kept under control as long as at least some of them, though probably never a majority, are inspired by a genuine belief in him personally and his cause. But this belief, even when it is subjectively sincere, is in very many cases really no more than the ethical "legitimation" of the desire for revenge, power, booty, and the rewards of office. And we must not let ourselves be persuaded otherwise about this, since the materialist interpretation of history is not a hansom cab to be picked up on an impulse, and it makes no exceptions for the agents

---

[83] The Red Guard was an armed militia recruited from the working class. They appeared first in Petrograd in the February Revolution in 1917, and their task was to guarantee public safety and defend the revolution.

of revolutions! But after the emotional excitement of revolution comes the return to the traditional *daily grind,* the hero of faith disappears, and, above all, faith itself evaporates or—and this is even more effective—becomes part of the conventional phrasemongering of political philistines and technicians. This process unfolds with particular rapidity in religious wars because they tend to be led or inspired by genuine *leaders,* prophets of revolution. For, as with every machinery of leadership, so here, too, one of the preconditions of success is that the followers undergo a process of spiritual impoverishment and routinization [*Versachlichung*], of a spiritual proletarianization in the interests of "discipline." Thus, when the followers of a man who fights for his faith come to power, they are particularly prone to degenerate into a very ordinary class of fortune hunters.

Anyone who wishes to engage in politics at all, and particularly anyone who wishes to practice it as a profession, must become conscious of these ethical paradoxes and of his own responsibility for what may become *of him* under the pressure they exert. For, I repeat, he is entering into relations with the satanic powers that lurk in every act of violence. The great virtuosos of unworldly goodness and the love of humankind, whether from Nazareth or Assisi or the royal palaces of India, have never operated with the methods of politics, that is, the use of force. Their kingdom was "not of this world," and yet they were and are at work in this world, and the figures of Platon Karatayev and Dostoyevsky's saints still remain their nearest successors.[84] Anyone who seeks the salvation of his soul and that of others does not seek it through politics, since politics faces quite different tasks, tasks that can only be accomplished with the use of force. The genius, or the demon, of politics lives in an inner tension with the God of love as well as with the Christian God as institutionalized in the Christian churches, and it is a tension that can erupt at any time into an insoluble conflict. People knew this even in the days of church rule. An interdict in those days represented a far more oppressive use of power over people and the salvation of their souls than what Fichte termed the "cold approval" of Kantian moral judgment.[85] Time and again the city of Florence was

---

[84] Platon Karatayev is the saintly plebeian in Tolstoy's *War and Peace* whose simple faith helps to restore the belief of the hero, Pierre Bezukhov, in his native land. The saintly characters Weber has in mind in Dostoyevsky must include Prince Myshkin in *The Idiot* and Alyosha Karamazov and Father Zossima in *The Brothers Karamazov.*

[85] According to Fichte, the moral life is based on the individual's consciousness of his duty. However, it can only be effective if this consciousness is backed up by a feeling that he refers to as "cold approval," in contrast to the "aesthetic feelings" of

placed under such an interdict, and yet its citizens continued to fight against the papacy. And in a reference to such situations in a beautiful passage from his *History of Florence*, if my memory serves me right, Machiavelli makes one of his heroes praise those citizens who esteemed the greatness of their native city more than the salvation of their souls.[86]

If you replace "native city" or "fatherland," terms that may not be utterly straightforward to everyone at the present time, with "the future of socialism" or "international peace," then you will be able to see the problem as it affects us today. For when men strive to attain such ideal goals by *political* action, they act in the name of an ethics of responsibility and make use of violent methods. In so doing they jeopardize the "salvation of their souls." But to seek such salvation through religious wars that are fought from the standpoint of a pure ethics of conviction is to risk damaging and discrediting their idols for generations to come, because the participants take no responsibility for the *consequences* of their actions. In such cases the political actors remain ignorant of the satanic powers that are at work. These powers are inexorable and create consequences for their actions and also subjectively for themselves, against which they are helpless if they fail to perceive them. "The Devil is old." And this does not refer to his age in years, to his time of life. "To understand him, best grow older."[87] I have never let myself be trumped in an argument by someone simply because he has claimed the privilege of greater age. But by the same token, the mere fact that someone is twenty and I am over fifty does not in itself convince me that his achievement should make me faint with admiration. Age is not the decisive factor here. What matters is the trained ability to scrutinize the realities of life ruthlessly, to withstand them and to measure up to them inwardly.

In truth, politics is an activity of the head but by no means *only* of the head. In this respect the adherents of an ethics of conviction are in the right. But whether we *should* act in accordance with an ethics of conviction or an ethics of responsibility, and when we

---

pleasure. *Das System der Sittenlehre nach den Principien der Wissenschaftslehre,* in *Johann Gottlieb Fichtes sämmtliche Werke,* vol. 4 (Berlin: Veit, 1845), p. 167.

[86] The passage occurs in a letter from Machiavelli to his friend Vettori. See Niccolò Machiavelli, *The Chief Works and Others,* translated by Allan Gilbert (Durham, NC: Duke University Press, 1989), vol. 3, p. 1150.

[87] This is a quotation from J. W. von Goethe, *Faust,* part 2, trans. by Philip Wayne (Harmondsworth: Penguin, 1959), p. 99, lines 6817–8.

should choose one rather than the other, is not a matter on which we can lay down the law to anyone else. We can only say one thing. We live in an age of excitement, which you may think is *not* of a "sterile" kind, though excitement is one thing, and it is not by any means always the same as authentic passion. Now in such an age, conviction politicians may well spring up in large numbers *all of a sudden* and run riot, declaring, "The world is stupid and nasty, not I. The responsibility for the consequences cannot be laid at my door but must rest with those who employ me and whose stupidity or nastiness I shall do away with." And if this happens, I shall say openly that I would begin by asking how much *inner gravity* lies behind this ethics of conviction, and I suspect I should come to the conclusion that in nine cases out of ten I was dealing with windbags who do not genuinely feel what they are taking on themselves but who are making themselves drunk on romantic sensations. Humanly, this is of little interest, and it fails utterly to shake my own convictions. By the same token, I find it immeasurably moving when a *mature* human being—whether young or old in actual years is immaterial—who feels the responsibility he bears for the consequences of his own actions with his entire soul and who acts in harmony with an ethics of responsibility reaches the point where he says, "Here I stand, I can do no other."[88] That is authentically human and cannot fail to move us. For this is a situation that *may* befall *any* of us at some point, if we are not inwardly dead. In this sense an ethics of conviction and an ethics of responsibility are not absolute antitheses but are mutually complementary, and only when taken together do they constitute the authentic human being who *is capable* of having a "vocation for politics."

And now, ladies and gentlemen, let us return to these questions *in ten years' time.* I fear, as unfortunately I must, that for a whole variety of reasons, an Age of Reaction will have long since broken in on us, and little will have been accomplished of what many of you, and I openly confess, I, too, have wanted and hoped for. Perhaps not exactly nothing at all, but at least, to all appearances, very little. This is highly probable. This will not disillusion me entirely, but, of course, it is an inner burden to have to live with this knowledge. If this proves indeed to be the case, then I would like to see what will have "become," in the inner sense of the word, of those of you who now feel yourselves to be "conviction politicians" and who share in

[margin note: i.e. 1929]

---

[88] Words historically attributed to Martin Luther at the Diet of Worms in 1521, explaining his refusal to recant his criticisms of the papacy.

the intoxication that this revolution involves. It would be wonderful if the situation then could resemble the one described in Shakespeare's sonnet 102:

Our love was new, and then but in the spring,
When I was wont to greet it with my lays;
As Philomel in summer's front doth sing,
And stops her pipe in growth of riper days.

But this is not the situation. What lies before us is not the "summer's front" but, initially at least, a polar night of icy darkness and harshness, whichever group may outwardly turn out the victor. For where there is nothing, not only will the kaiser have lost his rights but the proletarian will lose his rights, too. When this night slowly begins to recede, how many will still be alive of all those for whom the spring had seemed to bloom so gloriously? And what will have become of you all inwardly? Will everyone have become embittered or philistine, will they settle for a simple, dull acceptance of the world and their profession, or, and this is the third and not the most unlikely possibility: will they attempt a mystical escape from the world if they have the talent for it or—as happens frequently and damagingly—will they take to it against their better judgment because it is fashionable? In every such case, I shall conclude that they were *not* equal to the task they had chosen, *not* equal to the challenge of the world as it really is or to their everyday existence. They did not really, truly, and objectively have the vocation for politics in its innermost meaning that they had imagined themselves to have. They would have done better to cultivate neighborly contacts with other people, individually, in a simple and straightforward way, and apart from that, to go about their daily work without any fuss.

Politics means a slow, powerful drilling through hard boards, with a mixture of passion and a sense of proportion. It is absolutely true, and our entire historical experience confirms it, that what is possible could never have been achieved unless people had tried again and again to achieve the impossible in this world. But the man who can do this must be a leader, and not only that, he must also be a hero—in a very literal sense. And even those who are neither a leader or a hero must arm themselves with that staunchness of heart that refuses to be daunted by the collapse of all their hopes, for otherwise they will not even be capable of achieving what is possible today. The only man who has a "vocation" for politics is one who is certain that his spirit will not be broken if the world, when looked at from his point of view, proves too stupid or base to accept what he wishes to offer it, and who, when faced with all that obduracy, can still say "Nevertheless!" despite everything.

Name Index

Althoff, F., 48
Aphrodite, 23, 87
Apollo, 23, 87
Aquinas, St. Thomas, xiii
Arco-Valley, Count, xxxvi
Arendt, H., xxx (n.43), xliv
Aristotle, xliii, 1, 14
Arjuna, Prince, 87
Aron, R., xiv (n.16), xli (n.63), lix (n.116)
Augustine (St., of Hippo) lxi, 29
Ay, K.-L., xxxv (n.48)

Babich, B., xx (n.30), xxx (n.44)
Bacon, F., xxx, 15
Barclay, W., 52 (n.30)
Baudelaire, C., 22
Baumgarten, E., xix
Baxter, R., lviii
Bebel, A., 73
Bendix, R., xxix (n.42)
Berlin, I., xlvii–xlviii
Berman, M., lvii (n.110)
Bezukhov, P., 90 (n.84)
Birnbaum, I., xiii, xxxv
Bismarck, O. von, xi, liv
Brobjer, T., xx (n.30)
Brown, P., lxi (n.121)

Calhoun, J., 68
Chamberlain, J., 65–6
Chandragupta, King, 88 (n.81)
Charles V, Emperor, 45
Cleon, 54
Cobden, R., 67

Crusius, F., xxxv (n.49)

Dante, xxiv (n.38), 7 (n.9)
Disraeli, B., 63 (n.44), 66
Donatus, Bishop, lxi
Dostoyevsky, F., 85, 90
Durkheim, E., lix, lx (n.117)

Eden, R., xxxiii (n.45), lvii (n.109)
Eidin, F., xl (n.62)
Eisner, K., xxxiv–xxxvi, 80 (n.64)
Emerson, R. W., xxix (n.42),

Fichte, J. G., 84, 90
Foerster, F. W., 19, 86
Foucault, M., xlii (n.68)
Francis, St. (of Assisi), 82
Frauenstädt, J., 81 (n.68)
Freud, S., xi, xliii (n.73)
Friedrich, C., xvii

Galileo, 15
George, S., xxvii
Gerth, H., xli (n.64), xliii (n.70)
Gilbert, A., xlviii (n.83)
Gladstone, W., 65–7
Goethe, , J. W., xxvii, 3, 10, 27, 31 (n.32–3), 91 (n.87)
Goldman, H., xii
Guyer, P., 29 (n.28)

Hegel, G. W., xiv, xliv
Heidegger, M., xxix (n.42), xl (n.59)

Helmholtz, H., xxii, 6, 9
Hennis, W., xxii (n.33), xxxiii (n.45)
Henrich, D., xiv–xv, xli (n.67)
Hera, 87
Herman, B., xli (n.67)
Hollingdale, R., 17 (n.19), 35 (n.4)
Honigsheim, P., xiv (n.17)
Horowitz, A., xvii (n.23)
Hortsmann, R.-P., xli (n.67)
Humboldt, W. von, xxii
Hume, D., xv
Hung-chang, L., 50

Ihering, R. von, 9
Ilyich, I., 13 (n.15)
Indra, 87
Isaiah, 22, 31

Jackson, A., 68
Jaffe, E., xxxv (n.51), xxxvi
Jameson, F., lx (n.118)
Jaspers, K., xxix, xxx (n.43)
Jesus, 82
Justinian, Emperor, 51 (n.27)

Kant, I., xiv–xvii, xxxii, xliii (n.68), li, 28
Karamazov, A., 90 (n.84)
Karatayev, P., xlvii, 90
Kateb, G., xxix (n.42)
Kautilya, 88
Kimber, R., xxx (n.43)
Kissinger, H., xi (n.4)
Knies, K., xxvii (n.40)
Kohler, L. xxx (n.43)
Krishna, 87

Lash, S., xxxiii (n.45)
Laslet, P., lx (n.117)
Lassman, P., x (n.2), xix (n.28), xxi (n.32), xxiii, xlix
Leonardo, xxx, 15
Lehmann, H., xliii (n.72)
Lenin, V. I., xxxv, xl, xli (n.66), xliii (n.73), liv (n.97), lix, 84 (n.74)

Levy, C., xxxv (n.48)
Lichnowsky, xxxiv (n.47)
Liebersohn, H., xliii (n.72)
Liebknecht, K., xxxv, 74 (n.63)
Löwith, K., xiv (n.15), lvi (n.104)
Ludendorff, General, xi, xli
Lukács, G., 29
Luke, St., 23 (n.26)
Lukes, S., lx (n.117)
Luther, M., xlv, 31 (n.31), 83 (n.71), 86 (n.78), 92 (n. 88)
Luxemburg, R., xxxv, 74 (n.63)

Machiavelli, N., xlviii, 45, 84 (n.73), 88, 91
MacIntyre, A., xlvii
Maley, T., xvii (n.23)
Mande, A., 17 (n.20)
Marx, K., xi, xix, xxix, lvi–lvii, lix, lx (n.117), 38 (n.7)
Matthew, St., 23 (n.25), 81 (n.67), 82 (fn.69–70)
Mauss, M., lix (n.116)
Maximilian, Emperor, 44, 45 (n.15)
Mayer, A., xxxvii (n.55)
Mayer, R., 9
McCormick, S., xxxii (n.45)
Menger, C., xxii (n.33)
Merleau-Ponty, M., xl (n.60)
Michels, R., xliii, lx
Mill, James, 22
Mills, C. W., xli (n.64), xliii (n.70)
Mitchell, A., xxxiv (n.47)
Mitzman, A., x (n.3)
Mommsen, W. J., xiv (n.15), xxxvi (n.52), lix (n.113), lx (n.119), lxi
Montaigne, M., xv
Moore, G., xx (n.30), xxx (n.44)
Morgenbrod, B. xiv (n.15)

Naumann, F., xxxv
Nietzsche, F., ix, xi, xvii–xix, xxix–xxx, xxxii–xxxiv, xlii

(n.68), xliii (n.72), xlvii, lii–
liii, 17, 22, 35 (n.4)
Northcliffe, A., 56
Novalis, xvii

Oakes, G., lvii (n.107)
Osterhammel, J., lvii (n.107)
Ostrogorski, M., 63
Owen, D., xxxiii (n.45), xlii
(n.68), xliii (n.73)

Parsons, T., xii, liv (n.96)
Pericles, 54
Plato, xxx, 10, 14
Polt, R., xviii (n.24)
Puttkamer, R. von, 48

Ranke, L. von, xxiii, 6
Roscher, W., xxvii (n.40), lvii
Roth, G., xiv, xliii (n.72)
Rothermere, Viscount, 56 (n.39)
Runciman, W., lx (n.117)

Saner, H., xxx (n.43)
Scaff, L., lx (n.118–9)
Schäfer, D., xli, 19
Schiller, F., xvii
Schluchter, W., xiii (n.14), xiv
(n.15), xxi (n.32), xxxvi (n.52)
Schmoller, G., xxii (n.33), lvii
Schnädelbach, H., xxii (n.34)
Schnadhorst, F., 65 (n.49)
Schneewind, J., xli (n.67)
Schnitger, E., x
Schnitger, M., *see* Weber,
Marianne
Schön, M., lvii (n.107)
Schopenhauer, A., xvii, 81 (n.68)
Schroeder, R., xxvii (n.40), xxxiii
(n.45)
Schwab, A., xiii
Shakespeare, W., l, 93
Sica, A., x (n.1)
Simmel, G., 76
Small, R., xxx (n.44)
Socrates, 14, 31 (n.33)

Speirs, R., x (n.2)
Spener, P., 16
Strauss, L., xviii
Strong, T. B., xvii (n.23), xviii
(n.24), xxxiii (n.45), xxxviii
(n.57), xl (n.62), xli (n.63, 66),
xliii (n.73), xlvii (n.79), lii
(n.93)
Swammerdam, J., xxx, 15

Tacitus, 53 (n.36)
Tertullian, 29 (n.30)
Thoma, R., xxix
Tocqueville, A., xl (n.59)
Tolstoy, L., xxxi–xxxiii, xlviii, 13,
17, 27, 90 (n.84)
Treiber, H., xliii (n.72)
Trotsky, L., 33
Turner, B., xlii (n.68), lx (n.118)
Turner, S., xlix (n.85)

Uhland, L., 3

Vahland, J., xii (n.10), xiv (n.16)
Velody, I., xix, xxi (n.32), xxiii

Warren, M., xlii (n.68)
Washington, G., 67
Weber, A., xiii
Weber, E., x
Weber, H., x, xxxv (n.49)
Weber (née Schnitger), Marianne,
x, xi (n.6), xxxv (n.48)
Weber, Max (Sr.), x
Weierstrass, K., 10
Weiner, L., 17 (n.20)
Whimster, S., xxxiii (n.45), xxxv
(n.48)
Whitman, W., xxix (n.42)
Williams, B., xxxiii (n.46)
Wilson, W., xii
Wood, P., 29 (n.28)

Zarathustra, xlviii, liv, 17 (n.19)
Zossima, Father, xlviii, 90 (n.84)

Subject Index

academic career, ix, xxii–xxv, 1–2, 4, 7
administration, liv, lvii, 3, 32, 35–9, 44, 49–50
aesthetics, xlvi, 18, 29
allegiance, 34–6, 89
America, Americans, x, xxi–xxii, xxxvi, xlix, 1–5, 24, 42–4, 47, 62, 67–72, 75
aristocracy, aristocrats, lvii, 6, 18, 37, 49, 59
artists, art works, xxvii–xxviii, 9–11, 13, 15, 18, 29, 55
authority (*Herrschaft*), xix, xxxi, li–liii, lv, lvii–lviii, 34, 36–7

Bhagavad Gita, 87
Bolshevism, 59, 81, 85
Buddhism, Buddhists, 28
bureaucracy, xi, xl, li–lx, lxii, 2, 4, 24, 37, 43–5, 51, 63, 65
business, 3–4, 49, 65, 75, 80

cabinets, 46–8, 64, 66
cahiers de doléances, 52
Calvinism, xiii, 88
capitalism, xxix, liii, 3–4, 36, 69
career, *see* office
Catholicism, xiii, 88
caucus, 66–7
charisma, xi, l, liii, lxi, 34–5, 38, 62, 75
China 45, 49–50
Christianity, Christians, xxxiii, xlvi, liii, 23–4, 28, 51, 87–8, 90

classes (social), xi, lv–lvii, 59, 83
condottiere, 42
conflict, war, struggle, liv, xix, xxxiv–xxxvi, 46–7, 54, 79, 82, 85, 87
    of the Gods, 23, 26–7
    of worldviews, xlvii–xlviii, 22
conviction (politicians or parties of), xxxix, xliv, 83–6, 88, 91–2
culture, ix, xiv, xix, xxiii, xlvii, 11, 19–20, 23–4, 87

daemon, 31, 76, 86, 90
death, xxx, 13
demagogy, demagogues, 35, 53, 55, 63, 66–7, 81
democracy, liv, lvi, 6, 20, 24, 47, 53–4, 61, 65, 71, 75, 78
demos, 55
deus absconditus, 86
devil, 27, 91
dictator, dictatorship, 66–7, 74
dilettante(s), dilettantism, 45–6
diplomacy, 45, 50
disenchantment of the world, xx, xxx, xxxii, xliii, xlvi, lxi–lxii, 13, 30
doctors 41, 59

editors, 42
elections, liii, 5, 43, 58, 61–2, 68, 74–5; *see also under particular countries*

England, Great Britain, xlix, 47–8, 50–2, 55, 59, 62–4, 66–7, 74
entrepreneurs, 42, 61, 64, 69
erotic (the), 80
estates, 36–9, 49, 52, 59
ethic(s), xix–xx, xxxi–xxxiii, xlvii–xlviii, 22–3, 27
    and politics, xli–xlii, 70, 76–94
everyday(ness) 24, 41
experience, xi, xvii, xxvi, xxvii–xxviii, 8, 10–2, 15–6, 24, 30, 42
expert, expertise, 7, 10, 44, 46, 49

Florence, 90–1
following, *see* allegiance
France, French, 23, 43, 47, 51, 74
future, 80–1

gentry, 50–1
Germany, German, ix, xi, xxi–xxii, xxxiv–xl, xlix, liv, 1–4, 6, 23–4, 43, 48, 50, 54, 56, 62, 64, 66, 70, 72, 75, 78, 87
God, xiii, 16, 18, 23, 76, 83
    death of, xviii, xlviii
guilt, xxxv, 79–80, 83

holy, 77

idols, xx, 10, 91
India, Indians, 49, 51, 86–8, 90
intellectuals, intellectuality, ix, xiii, 53, 76–7
intoxication (*Rausch*), xxv, 8, 10, 77, 93
Italy, 44, 51

Jews, Judaism, 7, 28
journalists, journalism, 55–8, 60–1, 73, 76
jurisprudence, 18, 51

lawyers, 41, 51–3, 55, 59
leader, xi, xliii, xlix, lxi–lxii, 24–5, 32, 34–5, 41–2, 45–6, 49, 54–8, 61–4, 70, 73–5, 90, 93
legitimacy, xlix–l, liv–lv, lxi, 33–4, 36–8, 79
life, 10, 18, 24–5

Machiavellianism, 87
machines (political), 62–3, 65–8, 75
management *see* administration
ministers, 33, 42, 46, 61, 67, 69, 72

nation, xxxv–xxxvi, xxxix, liv, 80, 83
newspapers, 56
nobility, nobles, 50, 58
notables, notability, 59–65, 68, 71, 73

office, lii–liii, lv, 42–3, 51, 54, 64, 66, 68, 70–3, 76, 89

Parliament, parliamentary, liv, 35, 46–7, 52, 60–3, 64–9, 72–5
parties, 41–4, 47, 53, 57–70, 72–3
passion, xxvi–xxvii, xxix, xxxviii, xliii, lviii, 8–9, 54, 76–7, 92–3
peace 81–2, 85
philosophy, xix, xxxi, 26
political associations, clubs, xlviii, 60, 71
politicians, xxxix, 38–42, 49–50, 56–8, 60–1, 71, 75–8, 82
politics, xiii, xix, xxxi, xxxix, xliv, xlviii, xlix–l, lvi, 10, 19–20, 32–93
power, powerful, 53, 55, 58–9, 65, 72–3, 76–8, 80, 86, 89
    power politics, xxxix, 33, 78
    power holders 33, 38, 40, 46–8, 70
press (the), 56–7, 61

proletariat, 4, 52, 74, 93
prophets, lvii, 28–30, 35
Protestant, Protestantism, xi, xii,
    xiii, 16, 88,
Prussia, Prussians, 48, 55
Puritans, xiii, lviii

rational, xxix, liii–lvi, 12, 34, 51
rationalization, xx–xxi, xlvi, li–
    lvi, lviii–lxi, 12, 30, 51, 53
religion, religious, xxxiii, xlv, lv,
    16, 21, 24, 28–31, 64, 71, 78,
    83, 86–7, 89–91
Renaissance, 50, 89
rents, 39, 41
responsibility, xi, xxxix, xli, xlv–
    xlvi, 55–7, 73, 76–9, 82–6,
    90–1
revolution, ix, 52, 74, 76, 84–5,
    90, 93
Russia, ix, 59, 76

sacrifice of the intellect, 29, 31
science, xii–xiii, xix–xxi, xxiii,
    xxv, xxvii–xxxi, 1–31, 81
    and art, xxx, 15, 17
    and nature, xxx, 15, 17
    and the way to God, xxx,
        16–7
    and the way to happiness,
        xxx, xxxiii, 17
sciences (human), ix, 19
sciences (natural) 2–3, 15–6, 18
social democracy, social
    democratic parties, 55, 62–3,
    72–3

socialism, lx, 71, 84–5, 91
Spain, 43
specialization, xxv–xxvi, xlvi,
    lxii, 7–8, 12
spoils 68–9, 72
state, x, xxxv, xlix–liv, 3, 21, 32–
    4, 37–9, 41, 43–4, 46, 54, 56,
    59, 69
struggle *see* conflict
students, 1–3, 6–7, 19, 21, 24–5
Switzerland, 43

Tammany Hall, 62
technology, 18
theology, 16, 28–9
trade unions, 32, 73, 76

university, 20, 23, 25
    higher education, xxi–xxiii,
        1–6, 48
USA *see* America

vanity, 77
vocation, 35, 53, 75
vocation for politics, xxxiv–lxii,
    32, 40–1, 79, 92–3
vocation for science, xix–xxxiv,
    xxxvii, 5, 7–8, 14, 27

war, *see* conflict
workers, xxii, liii, 2–3, 41, 81

youth, youth movements, xiii, 8,
    10, 16, 24, 30